What Industry Leaders Are Saying About John
About the Martial Arts Business:

"In the thirty years I've known John Graden he has continually impressed me with his push to evolve as a person and a leader. Each decade he raises the bar to new heights. This book and his new organization are the latest pinnacles of an already groundbreaking career."
-- Joe Lewis: Former World Champion

"John Graden proves again he is a fighter, a proven leader and a damn good writer to boot. His new book goes way beyond business into an understanding of the martial arts instructor unlike anything ever written on the subject. This is a instant classic and required reading for anyone considering a career in the martial arts. It is no secret that John is a martial arts business guru, but few are aware of the fact that he won the Silver Medal in full contact kickboxing at the WAKO World Championships, the world's largest and toughest kickboxing event."
-- MikeAnderson: Founder, PKA and WAKO. Publisher, *Main Event* magazine

"Every time I think John Graden has reached the top of his profession, he surprises me. This book is the latest reason why Mr. Graden is considered the Teacher of Teachers. I was amazed at his insights in The Core Dynamics. No one understands martial artists like Mr. Graden."
-- Joe Brignoli: Former NAPMA Senior Consultant. President, Gold's Gym Karate

"I've studied everyone's information, but John Graden's work stands
above the rest for these reasons:
   1. He is a true martial artist and that is reflected in his teaching
   2. His information is easy to understand and interesting
   3. He prices everything to be affordable for even the smallest school
   4. He walks the talk when it comes to attitude
   5. He is a master motivator and a incredible speaker
These traits are never more apparent than in his new book, The Truth About
the Martial Arts Business. *This book will be required reading for all of my franchisees."*
-- Matt Fiddes: Founder of Largest Martial Arts School Franchisor. 5th Degree

"I love your no nonsense approach to sharing the truth about the martial arts business. This book will be mandatory reading for all my school owners and staff."
-- Terry Bryan, former General Secretary for the USA National Karate-Do Federation

I have just signed up for MartialArtsTeachers.com, and already I am amazed by the fantastic content. I have been a member of another organization for the last five years and with using the site I have found it to be much better than their package. I will be canceling them Monday.

-- Paul Kean , Skyaxe Blackbelt Academy, Dundee, Scotland

"I just got your new book and I couldn't put it down. Wow! I absolutely loved it. It has leapt into the top two on my list of all martial arts books.

I've always wanted to teach martial arts since my first class. I always thought that it wasn't possible to make a living teaching. Then I happened to order your Black Belt Management from Amazon. That has turned out to be one of the best decisions I've ever made. It came with your MATA business card. I have learned so much that I am ready to start teaching martial arts completely and establishing the first full time school in the area that doesn't close down or fail."

-- Andrew Lesmerises, Sterling, VA

"Your book is the most comprehensive book money can buy on the martial arts business. Anyone who wants to succeed in this industry must read this book. Sir, you are a man with vision; you are a leader; mentor; and are extremely knowledgeable on the subject of the martial arts business. You are the Teacher of Teachers in my book. Thank you for your insight."

-- Shihan Durand Howard, 7th Dan, Chief Instructor, Blue Life Karate Centers

"After reading the first 50-pages, I was so inspired that I drove to my school and started making the calls I should of been doing for the last 10 years. I even got one lead from 18 -months ago coming in next week. Your book has made me $1300 + in the first 50 pages.

By the way, who told you how I think act and why? Your insights are uncanny."

-- Eric Alex Jensen, XL Martial Arts Academy, Westcoast Australia

How can Mr. Graden identify so strongly with what I go through as an instructor in his book "The Truth About The martial Arts Business?" I was left thinking "he's talking about me.

This book should be in the hands of every instructor who wants the maximum potential out of their school."

-- Vincent Hopkins, Alperton, UK

"After reading John Graden's book, I have been able to fix key mistakes I've been making running my school. Using the solutions provided in his book, I am seeing positive results instantly.

He also writes this book as though he's speaking to you in person. As you get very practical information on running a successful martial arts school from his many years of experience and research, you also get entertained with his amusing anecdotes along the way!"

--Santanu Rahman, Kung-Fu for Holistic Health, www.kfhh.com

The Truth About the Martial Arts Business
John Graden

Also by John Graden

Black Belt Management
How to Open and Operate a Successful Martial Arts School
The ACMA Instructors Manual (Co-author)
The Martial Arts Q and A Book (Co-author)

Black Belt Management System (VHS/DVD/Audio CD)
1. How to Run a Black Belt School - Volume 1
2. How to Run a Black Belt School - Volume 2
3. Financial Control for School Owners
4. How to Develop a Powerful Black Belt Club
5. The Black Belt Club Upgrade
6. How to Develop a Leadership Team
7. Powerful Publicity Strategies
8. Internal Events for Profit and Retention
9. How to Develop a Great Staff
10. Communication and Leadership Skills for School Owners

Published by: Seconds Out, Inc.

Palm Harbor, FL

www.SecondsOutMedia.com

Copyright © 2006 Seconds Out,

Inc. All Rights Reserved

First Edition

Associations:

Copies of this book are available in quantity for use at a discount.

Write store@martialartsteachers.com or call 866-566-5426

Disclaimer

This book is designed to provide information about the subject matter covered. It is sold with the understanding that the publisher and author are not engaged in rendering legal, accounting or other professional services. If legal or other expert assistance is required, the services of a competent professional should be sought.

Running a martial arts school is not a get-rich-quick scheme. Anyone who decides to open a school must expect to invest time and effort into it with no guarantee of success.

Every effort has been made to make this book as complete and as accurate as possible. However, there may be mistakes both typographical and in content. Therefore, this text should be used only as a general guide and not as the ultimate source for school planning or operation. This manual contains information that is current only up to the printing date.

The purpose of this book is to educate and entertain. The author and publisher shall have neither liability nor responsibility to any person or entity with respect to any loss or damage alleged to have been caused directly or indirectly by the information in this book or its affiliated reports and/or websites.

Graden, John.

The Truth About the Martial Arts Business / John Graden -- Palm Harbor, FL : Seconds Out, 2006.

200 pages. Includes over 20 "historical" photographs

ISBN: 1-932835-01-6

1.†Martial arts--Business. 2.Karate--Training. 3.†Martial artists--Biography. 4.†Grade, John, 1960- .

Acknowledgements

The three years leading up to the publication of this book have been the most remarkable of my life. I've learned more about myself, our industry, family, and friends than all the previous years combined. My mother and father have been great through it all.

Please take a moment to help me show my appreciation for the people who have helped me to grow through this memorable period.

Writing a book is never easy, but my editors, Ana Hotaling and Janice Martin were a huge help in keeping me on track. Of course, the final step is to turn it over to my wife Lynette who has a keen eye and great suggestions.

As a teacher, my instincts are to share the lessons of my life. In this instance, this book is my classroom. In a sense, you could say the following are all part of the faculty.

The most important person on my team, in the growth of NAPMA, is one of my best friends, Scott Kelby. As my art director, he established new standards of quality that elevated NAPMA to a level never before seen in this industry. That accomplishment pales in comparison to the positive influence he has had on my life as a friend, entrepreneurial peer and trusted confidant. It was that quality that drove NAPMA's growth.

When you are tested and your friends, and family are unsure of your future, it's a fascinating process to watch how they respond. I am grateful that the response and support for me transitioning out of NAPMA far exceeded my most egotistical expectations. For the MATA members, friends and supporters that continue to back me and my efforts, my family offers you a deep bow of gratitude.

There is an old saying that you find out who your friends are during times of stress and, man do I have some great friends. Joe Lewis has been in my corner literally and figuratively for every round for more than 20 years. Mike Anderson is like a big brother and best friend to me. It's hard to imagine that it's been more than 20 years since a 17-year old gymnast named Kathy Marlor joined my white belt class. It's also hard to imagine an instructor being more proud than I am of her accomplishments with and beyond my influence. I'm proud to call Bob Wall my friend because we went from locking horns a few years back to locking arms together in the fight to help this industry. He has been a friend, champion and mentor for me.

Jeff Smith was my mentor in this business. He has always been a friend and wise counsel. He left a message of support on my telephone after the NAPMA mess that I will never forget.

I like to work with people I like. It's even better when I like them as friends before I work with them. Joe and Jennifer Galea are smart, fun and really good at what they do. They set a great example for all of us.

Don Warrener and I do some business together, but it's usually as an excuse to share our enthusiasm for the history of the arts and the insanity of the present landscape. Don is my reality check. Someone like me needs a friend like Don who has the confidence in our friendship to be brutally honest.

I am a martial artist. I love to fight and I love kata. I also believe in the law of attraction, which essentially says you bring people into your life who reflect what you think and care about. Tokey Hill, Kathy Long, Frank Shamrock, Walt Lysak, Richard Ryan, Jerry Jones, Dan Severn, and many more of what I call, "The nicest people who can kill you with their pinky" have been fantastic to me. I'm proud to call them all friends.

Some people have become good friends because they proactively reached out to help me grow MATA and personally contribute to the process. Thank yoMatt Fiddes, Charlie Foxman, Terry Bryan, Roland Jackson, Steve Stewart, Paul Reavlin, Brad Jones, George Alexander, Pablo Zamora, Ridley Able, Hersh Sandhoo, Jerry Beasley and all of the MATA Board members.

My fellow publishers have been very generous to me. A heartfelt thank you to Cheryl Angelheart, Mike DeMarco, Bill Bly, Rod Spiedel, Paul Clifton, Alfredo Tucci, Maurice Elmalem, Michael James and YK Kim.

Joe Brignoli has not only been in here with me growing MATA each day, but he was on the scene within minutes as my wife and her mother were helicopered from a horrible car accident. My four- and two-year old children would have been left there alone with strangers if not for his quick action and calming words. I don't have the words to express how much that means to us.

Finally, I am one of the few people I've ever known who looks forward to seeing his mother-in-law every day. She was seriously injured in that car accident with, among other ailments, a case of shingles that caused intense pain in the head 24 hours a day. Still, as always she led with a smile, took care of herself and by example, showed me a great lesson on dealing with adversity. To Rosaleen Houston: Cheers.

This book is dedicated to my wife and children Lynette, Alexander, and Christopher. Through them, I have experienced a dimension I never knew existed.

The Truth About the
Martial Arts Business

Table of Contents

This is the MAPro cover that I'm most proud of.
No single person has done more to educate and
motivate me than Brian Tracy.

Foreword
by Brian Tracy

The martial arts have played an important part of my life. Indeed, I attribute much of my success to the confidence and indomitable spirit I learned as a martial arts student when I was a young man. Character is important and few activities have the life-enhancing, character-building qualities of the martial arts. John Graden is a man of proven character.

I first met John Graden when he interviewed me in the mid-1990s. He was very familiar with my work and told me that his study of my material was the major source of information and inspiration for his success. It wasn't until I saw his presentation introducing his American Council on Martial Arts (ACMA) at the 1998 NAPMA World Conference that I realized he was not only a very successful and influential martial artist but also clearly a man of vision.

The ACMA - now the MATA Instructor Certification Course - was the right program at the right time. While John's NAPMA pioneered the business of running a school, the ACMA was created with one purpose in mind: to make sure the interaction between the instructor and student remains as safe and professional as possible.

In a fragmented field such as the martial arts, the creation of the ACMA was a daunting task and he pulled it off. I was proud to be a board member of the program and continue to support the idea. Simply put, all the business skills in the world can't make up for poor service. If you are going to be a martial arts professional, be the best.

From the remarkable success of NAPMA and ACMA to his Martial Arts Teachers' Association, John Graden has met his challenges head on with the integrity and character of a champion.

A world-caliber martial artist, John Graden has combined his high technical standards and superb teaching skills with proven business systems to show you how to succeed in *The Truth About the Martial Arts Business*.

Brian Tracy
www.BrianTracy.com

The Truth About the
Martial Arts Business

Preface

This is my third book on the martial arts business. The first two, *Black Belt Management* and *How to Open and Operate a Successful Martial Arts School*, are still excellent sellers and are as relevant as ever. Both have even been adapted as college textbooks.

I am a teacher by nature, and that is what I enjoy doing most. My third book, the *ACMA Instructors' Certification Manual*, was not about the martial arts business itself; it was about how to teach in a more professional, safe manner. That program is now the MATA Instructors' Certification program.

This book addresses what kind of person becomes a martial arts teacher and how those traits can help or hurt us as professionals. I very much like martial artists, as they are far and away the most interesting, diverse, and colorful group of people you could meet. As different as our styles and backgrounds may seem, however, we are all more alike than we are different. That subject fascinates me, and I hope you will enjoy exploring it with me.

Regardless of style, location, or background, many martial arts instructors have in common spending their career mired in a conflict. They portray themselves as being "true to the arts" or "champion of all time," while struggling desperately for students.

What are the symptoms of this common affliction?

Cussing the "McDojo" across town, while advertising "No Contracts!"

Berating the "Belt Factory" down the street that boasts three times the students even at three times the tuition.

Surrounding himself with a core group of five guys and one girl who would train with him in the parking lot at 5 a.m. and pointing to them as a measure of success.

Here is the interesting part: Most of us have shown all three symptoms. I certainly have. A guy in my town named Michael Kinney could not have been nicer to me, but I viewed him as a belt factory. In retrospect, I realize he was an entrepreneurial guy who was also a decent black belt. He had an advertising background, and, in my naive opinion as a young black belt, he oversold himself. He was nice to me; I was not nice to him. My loss.

My instructor Walt Bone was quite different. Odds are he would have called Mr. Kinney out for a high-noon duel. Years before, when Mr. Bone was hired to teach a college class and I was the assistant instructor, there was another instructor on campus. Mind you, there was no real competition, as they were paid the same regardless of the number of students. Anyway, this guy arranged a meeting with Mr. Bone. Afterwards, Mr. Bone admitted to me he went there prepared "to beat the guy's ass." But he was taken aback by the other guy's genuine effort to help him acclimate to the college. Mr. Bone was not used to competing instructors helping each other out.

Old habits die hard and are inherited by the next generation – in this case, your author. I was Mr. Bone's highest-ranking black belt. It would be fair to say that, of his "golden children," I shined brightest. He had a lot of good black belts, but I was the most serious addict. I totally embraced the martial arts life. I devoured Funakoshi's books, absorbed *Enter the Dragon*, and read Joe Lewis articles until the pages crumbled.

I share the following only because so many of you will read this and immediately recognize your own past to some degree. Keep in mind that I loved my instructors. Each had a different influence on me that has made me the martial artist I am.

First, some context. When I was 10 I attended a Largo Blue Devils peewee football team tryout. The coach said, "Graden! Get in there and play tackle!" I didn't know what a tackle was. I thought you were supposed to tackle the guy with the ball. I didn't know there was a position called tackle. Needless to say, I didn't do well. Because I didn't "perform to his expectations," the coach grabbed me by my helmet mask and shook it while screaming at me. Now, some contrast. Hank Farrah and Walt Bone taught my first martial arts class, with Mr. Bone doing most of the talking. He was impressive as a teacher, and the subject matter blew my mind. When he asked if I had any martial arts experience, I suffered a major flashback to my days with the Blue Devils. When I confessed I had no experience, Mr. Bone said, "Good. Bring your feet out as wide as your shoulders. This is called shoulder-wide. Bend your knees . . ." I had never had a teacher of any subject relate to me this way. I may not have had martial arts experience, but I could follow directions.

I'll never forget when he taught me the logic of a straight punch. That was huge! At that early time martial arts was, for me, all about logic and physics, and it just made so much sense.

Hank Farrah took me as his personal training partner when I was a 14-year-old green belt. Each day I came in to clean the school. Technically, that was how I earned my tuition, but, in fact, it was my first labor of love. While cleaning the school each day was my duty for lessons, it was also my escape from a house full of tension and intimidation. Best of all, it put me in the company of my instructors all afternoon. I would clean and then practice each day.

Mr. Farrah recognized in me a desire to learn and an ability to endure. He came by my house after school and picked me up in his sports car. We would go to the school and train. Of course, that meant I would hold the target for his 10 kicks on each side, and he would hold it for five of mine. It didn't matter. I was training with the "Suntan Superman." I could not have had a better influence at the time. Mr. Farrah was fit, always smiling, with charisma to burn.

As a blue belt, I began teaching private lessons. When I earned my black belt in 1978 at age 17, the school hired me for $5 per class. My goal was to be just like my instructors.

When my instructor told me that exams happened only when he felt enough of us were ready to test, that was law. When the board break requirements for a brown belt exam were punching two boards (no palm heel here), round kicking two boards, and doing a running jump side kick over two people through three boards, that was law.

Those are just a few of the operational "laws" that I learned as a young boot, as new black belts were called. As in many instructor/student relationships, these so-called laws are revealed to the young student with the sense that each instruction is part of the Ancient Wisdom or The Way for which the martial arts is renowned. Let me clue you in on that one: They are not. A great example of this was in the days when a tournament promoter would pull all the black belts into a room for a "rules meeting." This always deteriorated into a huge argument because everyone had their own set of "laws." We'll explore more of how (and why) we are governed by these inherited laws in The Core Dynamics section.

Mr. Farrah left the school shortly before I earned my black belt, so I worked exclusively with Mr. Bone. His teaching methods and the procedures he taught me spanned the entire spectrum from excellent to, well, not so excellent.

Every one of the laws and attitudes I adopted helped me form a strong base as a martial artist, but many of them were antiquated, dumb dungeon dojo methods that it took me years to shed. It certainly wasn't Mr. Bone's fault. He was simply teaching as he had been taught in the

Tex Kwon Do days of Blood and Guts that came out of his instructor Allen Steen's remarkable family tree which, of course, started with Jhoon Rhee.

I don't want this book to duplicate what I have done with MATA, NAPMA, ACMA, *MAPro*, and my other books. However, I've noticed that, even with all the information out there, many veteran school owners still struggle. Yet, I see guys like my friend Matt Fiddes in the UK who, in his mid-20s, has already become a martial arts millionaire by studying my material and others. Why do men and women like Matt apply the information while others don't? We will explore this in the first section, "The Core Dynamics."

The second section will discuss very specific how-to information for opening and running your martial arts school.

This book covers the areas that have been dominating my thoughts for the past five years:

1. Why, with all of the information out there now, are guys still resisting what has proven to work?
2. What are the most common questions about how to run a school?

This is *The Truth About the Martial Arts Business*. I hope you enjoy it.

The Truth About the
Martial Arts Business

Introduction
What is a Martial Arts Professional?

When I created *Martial Arts Professional* magazine, I purposely put Martial Arts before Professional. In my view, the martial arts come first. Very few school owners are "professional" before they are martial artists. Even those from corporate or professional backgrounds have a difficult time translating that experience into a martial arts school. I have never met anyone who joined a martial arts school with the intent of opening his own school. People don't join a martial arts school as a career path. Again, the Martial Arts precede the Professional.

This is a unique business. I liken it in many ways to show business, in that the conflux of art and money creates a tremendous amount of confusion, delusion, and insecurity.

In all areas of art, there is a struggle between the integrity of your art and the economic realities of Western culture. A rock band may be pushed by a record label to create hits, when their real passion and talent is in music of more depth and consequence. A serious, well-trained actor may take a formula action film role for fun and money, yet face ridicule for "wasting her talents on drivel." A world-champion kickboxer may pass a child on a belt exam, rather than lose the student's tuition if he drops out or, worse, face the wrath of the mother. Most black belts would rather climb in the ring against a Frank and Ken Shamrock tag team than face a livid mother who knows better than you what a blue belt should look like.

So, what is a Martial Arts Professional? It's someone who is teaching for money. Regardless of how much money or to what degree it represents your total income, if you are asking people for money in exchange for your knowledge, you are a professional.

This book is for those who accept that, if we are going to ask for money, we have an obligation to our students to become the best professional possible. This is an important attitude, and I bring it up in the beginning because, if you do not accept that running a school is first

19

and foremost a business, then all the strategies and techniques you learn will be of little use.

Our industry does not need another black belt boasting that he teaches only authentic martial arts and that everyone else is a belt factory. This is what I call the "Higher Purpose Defense," when a guy lacks either the skill or the confidence to build a strong, thriving, profitable school, so he falls back on an altruistic cop-out. He says he's not a sell-out or that he teaches true martial arts and that the other schools are just McDojos. He is taking the Higher Purpose Defense. However, if I could wave a magic wand and give this guy 300 students and $40,000 a month gross, his new higher purpose would be the higher gross. This is the delusion I referred to above.

Online polls from the Martial Arts Teachers' Association website (www.martialartsteachers. com), indicated that, out of more than 500 responses, more than 58 percent grossed less than $7,500 per month in their schools; 48 percent charged less than $80 per month; 51 percent earned less than $40,000 from teaching. This tells us there is plenty of room for growth.

Here is an interesting point. Odds are that, even at these low levels, some of these instructors are already overpaid. There are still plenty of dungeon dojos out there. We don't need more. Of course, there are also people who teach part-time and never plan to go full-time.

But I can say this with a lot of certainty: Most of these respondents are underpaid. Most are good black belts who simply need a system, some encouragement, and then some accountability. This book and my programs are designed to help owners break out of these levels and earn rewards in line with their contributions to the community. For instance, our Quantum Leap Program groups owners into teams that meet every 90 days to share stats, train together, grow together, and hold each other accountable for execution over the previous 90 days. Our first goal in the QLP is to get our members to a six-figure income.

Of course, some owners will reach that level without my help and that's great. However, most owners will accomplish it much faster with some help and support.

Our industry will grow when black belts commit to learning how to teach age-specific classes professionally and safely – when they support those teaching skills with ethical, proven business systems that add value to the student's experience and to the owner's own bottom line. None of that is part of anyone's black belt exam. Earning a black belt is just the ticket to get into the school. My books, the Martial Arts Teachers' Association, and our Quantum Leap Program are a great school. Let's get started.

I was a third-degree brown belt in this photo taken at a 1975 karate school picnic.
The gi is dirty because we played football all afternoon.

**The Truth About the
Martial Arts Business**

Section One
The Core Dynamics

When I created NAPMA in 1994, there was little good information available to the industry as a whole. Owners were struggling because they simply didn't know any way of running a school other than the system they inherited from their instructor, which we know is usually a recipe for disaster.

NAPMA gave you a way to learn how to run a school. I created *Martial Arts Professional* magazine to help the entire industry, even non-NAPMA members, by exposing them to methods, systems, people, and ideas that had proven successful. Now, MATA does the best job of all, because the entire library is updated three to four times a week. This massive resource is at your fingertips 24/7.

Still, as time went by, I found it fascinating to observe that two school owners – in the same styles, general markets, and circumstances, and exposed to the same information – might react very differently. One would prosper with it, and the other wouldn't even try it. After more than a decade of study and exposure to this great information, why were some schools still struggling, while others thrived?

The answer is Core Dynamics. We martial artists are a unique group but, as school owners, we face the same challenges. More importantly, we all have the same Core Dynamics.

Core Dynamics of the Professional Martial Artist define the underlying forces that control our patterns of thought and behavior. Nearly every martial arts professional has the same obstacles, but the distinction is how the top school owners in the world deal with them. How an instructor or school owner deals with the Core Dynamics determines his or her success.

Before we get into the how-to, I'm going to help you understand some of the obstacles that may be holding you back. It's important for you to understand why you do or don't do something. I want you to be the one who grows instead of stagnates.

First, we'll examine a common pathway to opening a school and the predictable patterns of thought and behavior in most of our backgrounds. Then, we will contrast how the top owners deal with the Core Dynamics versus struggling school owners.

1. The Control Factor
2. Finding Your Voice
3. Value What You Do
4. Clarity of Purpose
5. Black Belt Eyes

585-4462   393-1285

FLORIDA KARATE ACADEMY
BEGINING CLASS TIMES
MON. & WED. 6-7
TUES. & THUR. 8:30 - 9:30

My instructors (left to right) Hank Farrah, Debbie Bone, Walt Bone, and Richard Jenkins in 1973. Though they were outstanding black belts and teachers, each had his own rules on everything from how to run a school and what it means to be a black belt. The Control Factor and Black Belt Eyes were in full force at this school.

I was so enthused with my karate school, I wanted everyone to join. I used to leave their business cards everywhere. My eighth-grade teacher told me to stop leaving them on his desk.

Chapter One
The Control Factor

Here in the Tampa Bay area – the 12th largest TV market in the U.S. – the local CBS TV affiliate did a three-part series called "Black Belt Scandals." The series exposed a local instructor who had Wite-Out® on his rank certificate. You could see a 3 was replaced with a 7. He even had a fake chiropractor's certificate on the wall.

Though this guy was giving neck and back adjustments to students, including children, the chiropractic college reported he had never attended the school. Next, the reporter contacted his martial arts association. They had no record of him. Mind you, I'm less than confident of martial arts associations' record keeping, but it looked very bad.

As a demonstration, the reporter applied to another martial arts organization for a black belt certificate, which was promptly mailed to her. She made it clear that all she had to do was send in $25 and she was recognized as a black belt, without ever having taken a martial arts lesson in her life.

She then purchased a black belt at a local martial arts supply store and took the certificate and belt to the business licensing office. When asked what was needed to open a martial arts school, the lady behind the counter said, "Pay $35 for a business license. That's it."

The reporter looked into the camera and remarked that, though she had the belt and the certificate, they were useless because she didn't need them to open a school. She dumped them both in the trash.

I was on a 10-day tour of Italy with the WAKO USA Team when this happened. When I got back, it was the talk of Tampa Bay.

Beyond exposing a lack of ethics in the martial arts industry, the story illustrated that there are no educational or, for the most part, licensing prerequisites to open a martial arts school in the United States. In the United Kingdom, Canada, and other countries there are some rudimentary licensing requirements, usually having to do with CPR and general safety. There is very little required that is specific to the martial arts.

To be clear, I am not calling for any type of government regulation. I created the ACMA (now the MATA Instructor Certification Program) as a way of educating instructors on teaching methods that are accepted and proven universally by the highest academic standards worldwide. My goal has always been that we raise our own standards of performance and teaching. That is a tough road in this industry, and we will explore why in this section.

There is little question that our industry has a very low barrier to entry. The range of people opening martial arts schools is vast. Some people open schools after graduating college with an MBA, while others have just been released from prison. The good side is that martial artists are as diverse a group as you can find in any field. The most colorful, interesting people I've met in my life have been martial arts instructors. The downside is obvious: like any profession, the indiscretions made by a minority of unethical instructors make it harder for all of us to be taken seriously as professionals.

When researching why some owners take the material and apply it while others let it stack up in their office, my first thought was that owners with higher education probably did better growing a school. However, in the next moment I realized that couldn't be true. I certainly didn't have a business background when I opened my school, and my GED didn't exactly speak to high education. Yet I earned a six-figure income as a school owner in the early 1990s. The fact there are no educational prerequisites allowed me to get started in the first place.

I believe the difference lies in our collective background as martial artists. Keep in mind that the Core Dynamics are unique to those of us who have embraced the rigors of training far beyond those of our classmates. We didn't just train hard; we made the martial arts our life. Many of us endured beatings, mental abuse, and insane requirements to move up the rank ladder to our black belt and beyond. We stuck it out while our classmates struck out. In appreciation for all that hard work, our instructors often found ways to abuse our loyalty. Who the heck puts up with that? We did.

I was lucky that my instructors never abused my loyalty. Every instructor I worked with – Hank Farrah, Walt Bone, and Joe Lewis – took me under his wing and made me a protégé. But, as the head of the world's largest martial arts professional association, I've heard countless

The Truth About the
Martial Arts Business

horror stories of master instructors abusing the loyalty of their top students. Guess who tend to be the top students? Guys and girls like you and me.

Who are we? We are probably the only students in our white belt class that actually made black belt. My first night in karate class, Mr. Bone explained that less than four percent of us would make brown belt and that less than two percent of us would make black belt. I understood that he was challenging us to overcome the odds. I too feel black belt shouldn't be easy, and I am a firm believer that pain is part of the training. I don't dispute that. I am more curious about why we endured while others dropped out. What relation is there between our endurance and running a school as a business?

We Have Similar Backgrounds

Regardless of our style or where we began to train, we martial arts school owners have similar backgrounds and motivations. I've discussed this with hundreds of black belts and a number of psychologists. Herein lies the genesis of the Core Dynamics.

Why did we first join a martial arts school? Chuck Norris tells how having an alcoholic father was a major motivator for him to get into martial arts, and I think most career black belts have had a similar experience. Most of us joined a martial arts school because we had been bullied, beaten, or in some way intimidated or powerless for a long time, typically in our youth. This common denominator has a massive effect on our industry, not as much from a marketing standpoint as from a causation standpoint.

An industry run by people out of oppressed, intimidating situations but who now see themselves as powerful "masters of the martial arts" is unique. It's convoluted. As beneficial as it is for the individual, the transition from powerless to powerful in the martial arts often creates a new set of baggage.

Most of us got into the martial arts because we were personally bullied, beaten, intimidated, and/or mistreated, or we were in an environment of tension, violence and/or abuse, particularly as kids.

Interestingly, if you study successful people, a common theme is either mental or physical hardship or abuse as a child. Bill Clinton's dad too was a raging alcoholic. Ted Turner's dad arranged to blow his own brains out at a time he knew Ted would be the first to find him, so he could clean up the mess before his mom got home.

Maybe your dad hit your mom, or your brother beat you, or you were the target of bullies. Whatever the situation, the end result was that you found yourself in a threatened place for an extended period of time. It was not your fault. You were just a kid. According to the doctors I've talked with, this creates a feeling of powerlessness because the scary things that are happening to you are out of your control. If you're in such a situation for an extended period of time, the martial arts present an escape and a way to gain power and respect.

If you joined a martial arts school in the 1970s like me, odds are your school was a dungeon dojo: a smelly place where students were "tortured" in the name of discipline. In these schools we discovered a world where beatings happened, but with a kind of perverse logic.

There were clear rules and boundaries. Rather than a lack of control, the martial arts are all about control. If you took the beatings, followed the rules, and practiced your techniques, your rank within the organization would rise. With each step up the rank ladder, you moved closer to the inner circle of the school, which translates to the big R word: Respect.

Respect is *the word* in the martial arts. Because a kid gets little of it, especially in the kind of environment described above, respect is very attractive. One of the first lessons you're taught in martial arts school is respect. It is also clear that respect is related to rank. That's a natural and necessary hierarchy in the martial arts, but boy is it appealing to a person who has been beaten down one way or another.

As a kid, you can't choose your school, your parents, your city, your neighborhood, or much of anything else about your environment. You have no control and, when the situation is negative and intimidating, that debilitating feeling can stick with you for life. Martial arts changes all that. The rank system provides a direct path to respect that you control by training hard, following the rules, and enduring.

With rank comes more respect and control, to the point that people bow to you and call you Sir or Ma'am. Because you trained the hardest and absorbed the lifestyle without question, it's usually not long before you are helping out in class and then actually leading classes. To a kid who was in an intimidating, powerless situation, this turnaround in control is like water to a plant: it gives new life. I know it did for me. Being a teacher of anything gives you a feeling of significance and self esteem.

I was in 8th grade when I earned my green belt. Green is a great belt color, because it's a lot darker than orange or yellow. It looks like you've been around for a while and know something.

After I cleaned the school, Mr. Farrah said that now that I was a green belt, we were going to *rank spar* for three rounds. This, I discovered, was the instructor's way of making sure you didn't get too cocky with your new belt. For three rounds he pounded me into the ground.

Then Mr. Bone drove up. He said, "Hey, green belt. Let's belt fight." I said I had just rank sparred with Mr. Farrah. He laughed and said we were going to fight using our belts like nunchaku. The rule was no hitting to the face and, if your opponent grabbed your belt, you could punch and kick them until they let go (you can view one of these belt fights at www. martialartsteachers.com's *Truth About the Martial Arts Business* section).

I really had no choice, so I bowed in by snapping my belt between my hands with a hard yank. He did the same, and that's when I noticed something. My snap sounded kind of soft. His sounded like a whip snapping, because his belt was one of the heavy Tokaido silk black belts, whereas mine was made of very soft, light cotton. I was in big trouble.

He hit me on the outside of the thigh so hard I almost flipped. My attempts to hit him fluttered into his blocks. He continued to hit me in the same spot over and over until the skin was broken and I was bleeding and limping while trying to fend him off. After we bowed out, I took my green belt class and staggered home. The next day on the school bus, every time we hit a bump, my eyes would water from the pain in my body, especially my thigh. As painful as that was, I knew it was a reward for moving up the ranks. I was moving closer to the inner circle, and it was worth it.

In my school, white belts were called "scummy white belts." You didn't have a name until you got up to at least blue or brown belt (oddly enough, you were given a key to the school when you made blue belt, so that you could practice). Until then, you were referred to by your rank, as in "Green belt, get over here." In my case, since I cleaned the school for lessons, the instructors knew me well.

Despite the pain involved in this type of training, many of us took to it like a moth to light. Karate class was a haven to me. From my first day in class at age 13, I knew this was what I was going to do for the rest of my life. Since I had quit football, and karate required a 12-month contract for $25 per month, my parents wouldn't pay for the classes, so I cleaned the school for lessons. I was the original "wax on, wax off" kid. I remember the second day I was cleaning. Mr. Farrah snapped at me to finish my cleaning before I practiced. With a flashback of being yelled at by my parents and embarrassed in front of other kids, I almost quit that day.

I remember making the conscious decision not to fall back into the pattern of quitting if things got rough. The following week he punched me in the head with his bare fist. It was playful, not malicious, but it really hurt. I was getting his attention, so I took it.

Mr. Farrah was a great influence on me during my teen years. Mr. Farrah was a funny, charismatic guy who mentored me all the way to first-degree brown belt. He taught me a lot but there were clear rules and no doubt who the black belt was.

The Golden Child

In time, like me, many of you became the "golden child" of the school. You trained harder than anyone, and you were the best or one of the best students in the school.

By the time I was a first-degree brown belt, I rarely lost a sparring match against anyone other than my instructors. In fact, I refused to test for black belt, because it didn't mean anything to me at the time. Keep in mind, this was a time of massive change in the martial arts. Full contact had begun, and many of the myths of the "deadly black belt" were being exposed as nothing more than fable. Forms were being questioned as useless, as many black belts were shown to be only average fighters reduced to desperate, wild swinging brawlers in the full-contact arena.

After Mr. Farrah left the school, I stopped coming to my brown belt class. I would show up at the end of the class when they were getting ready to spar. I would walk out onto the floor, spar, and then leave. My instructor, Walt Bone, who was an excellent black belt and teacher, finally expelled me from the school.

Nine months later, he let me back in, and I returned to the arts with a deeper appreciation of what they were. I have worked hard ever since to honor them. I became Mr. Bone's highest-ranking black belt until his death in a plane crash on December 16, 1982 (in a strange twist, I took him to the airport when he flew home to Dallas to visit his mom over the holidays. When I got home, I told my roommate, "I will never see him again." Just a week later he died in a small plane crash in Texas).

These stories illustrate the path that many of us have traveled. It typically starts with an extended state of being powerless and out of control. That's our motivation to join the martial arts school. Though intimidation and violence existed within the school, the traditions and rules made it more meaningful, and we endured the pain to move into the inner circle. In the martial arts that inner circle is earned by gaining rank, which wins you Respect.

You Begin Teaching

If you are an instructor today, odds are that you began teaching classes for your instructor shortly before or after you earned your black belt. You became a good teacher, but you were still under the control of your instructor, and you loyally taught and followed his syllabus.

This is usually a great period in our lives. We can teach without risk but, more importantly, we have gained control of a very important part of our new life and are in a position of power. People bow to us and call us Mr. or Ms. or a title of some sort that we associate with prestige, such as "Sensei." That's a big turnaround for many of us. That is the beauty of the martial arts. The arts provide you with a healthy way of redefining yourself and your future.

I was an 18-year-old bus boy clearing tables in a restaurant during the day and Mr. Graden, black belt teacher, at night. My days were filled with, "Graden, clear off table six, fast!" My nights were, "Mr. Graden, would you please speak to my son? He's having trouble in school, and he looks up to you so much . . ." Which do you think appealed to me and fueled my ambition? I know which appealed to you, because this book is not about how to clear tables.

Implied Wisdom

If you started your training in the 1970s, or maybe even the 1980s, because of the *Kung Fu* TV show and the many *Kung Fu* movies, there was what I call an "implied wisdom" in earning a black belt. As a black belt, especially a "master," you were perceived as somehow knowing more about life than the average person. This image of the martial arts master as being a master of life was reinforced by the martial arts movies, television shows, and magazines.

To this day, that prestige has tremendous pull and attraction for martial artists. Why do you think black belts seem in such a rush to call themselves Master, Grand Master, Senior Master, or Supreme Grand Master? In the real world we have master mechanics, master sergeants, chess masters, and even chess grandmasters, but only martial artists insist on actually being called "Master."

On the popular TV show *Seinfeld*, a small-time conductor insisted everyone, including his girlfriend, call him "maestro." I wonder if sometimes we don't generate some laughs ourselves with these titles.

Everything is Under Control

At some point while you were dutifully teaching classes for your instructor, I bet a few students and/or parents let you know that they preferred your classes to those of your instructor. At first, you thought they were just being polite, but then you began to notice things your instructor did that you would not do 'if it were your school.'

You enjoyed the attention and the rewards that came from teaching martial arts. Maybe the martial arts school became your social circle because it was easy for you. You were moving up in rank, training hard, and teaching, which automatically earned you respect and recognition within this community. Meeting people is easy when you outrank them.

You were loyal to your instructor and strongly believed in what you taught, because these techniques and methods brought you out of the darkness of intimidation to being a revered black belt instructor.

It was natural that we developed deep emotional ties to the techniques and the methods of our school. The mere mention of our school, style, or organization brought on fierce feelings of pride. This is also why the suggestion that there may be a better or a different way is met with initial resistance. These connections are so strong they are even parodied in films, because the "my kung fu is better than yours" scene has been played to death in movies. When an art has changed our life, it's not always easy to admit that it may be flawed in some degree or way.

It's Not Just You

While you were teaching for your instructor, you may have suggested new ways of doing things, including teaching, testing, and marketing, but virtually every idea of yours was shot down. Your instructor had everything in his control, and trying something new was a risk he was not willing to take. I understand wanting to stay in your comfort zone. I was certainly that way. Once, as a school owner, I wanted to introduce some energy into classes by clapping in between drills or forms. I literally stayed up at night, thinking through how to introduce this concept. I was afraid my students would think I'd gone sissy and walk out.

Teaching martial arts is nirvana for a control freak. By the time you become a black belt following the path I've just described, you are a full-fledged control freak. You control how students move, breathe, where they look, what they should think about and, even in some extreme cases, some spiritual aspects of their lives. So, to risk giving up control for even a minute was very tough for me. This clapping thing became a huge obstacle for me. After all, my instructors would have never done something like this.

I chickened out during the first two classes and decided I would do it in the last class of the night, which was my brown and black belt class. I figured, if it bombed, only they would see it (by the way, don't introduce new ideas to your advanced students first. They like things the way they are now. That's why they are here. Some of them have developed deep connections to the way things are, just as you did at that rank).

I had the class do a form, Tan Gun, as a warm up. I was thinking, OK, after this form, I'm going to do it. But, instead of simply saying, "Hey! Give yourself some energy!" and clapping to show them what I meant, I used the classic control-freak method. When they finished the form, I snarled, "Attention!" Everyone snapped to. "Extend your left hand!" Every left hand popped out. "Extend your right hand!" Every right hand popped out. "Clap!"

I had to be in total control of every step of the way to clapping. It was silly. They did it and liked it, and it became part of our school's energy, but without the micro-managing from me to extend each hand like robots. Much of our hesitation and fear of new ideas and changes are rooted in this control factor. You've gained control of your situation, and you are afraid of trying something new that might put you out of control, even for a moment.

The Beginning of the End

In moving from student to school owner, a few things may have happened to you as the teacher. Your instructor may have been "overusing" you and taking advantage of your loyalty. This is never pleasant, because you have to face some cold, hard realities, and your relationship with your instructor begins to change. Your spouse, family, or friends may have suggested that you were being exploited. They may have urged you to open your own school. Perhaps even a student offered to back you financially.

Being loyal, you decided to be upfront with your instructor and tell him you were considering opening a school. What was his reaction? Either he went for your throat or insisted you pay him a percentage of your lifetime earnings.

Why did he react that way? Odds are, because he went through the same cycle of moving from no control to total control about a decade before you, and then you threatened that control. He had you, his golden child, teaching classes. You symbolized his success as an instructor, but now you were making the biggest decision in your martial arts life without his control? Not without a fight you weren't.

This is often the beginning of the end of your relationship with your instructor. If he can't control you, he may perceive you as disloyal. Does this sound familiar? "I taught you everything you know. You owe me! How dare you take what I taught you and use it against me?" Mind you, he will probably view anything less than totally capitulating to his demands as working against him.

Contrast this with a college professor. If you attend law school, your law professor wants nothing more than for you to go out and be successful using what he taught you. That is his reward. He doesn't ask for a percentage of your revenue.

One school owner would bring each student into his office right before he tested for black belt. He pulled a .38 revolver out of his drawer, set it on the desk, and explained, "Just to be clear. You will never, ever open a martial arts school in my area. Understood?"

Conflicting Goals

When you finally open your own school, the control factor continues to be an influence. For instance, maybe you attend one of my Fast Track Programs. In our phone session, you learn how important it is to make follow-up calls to people who have inquired about your school but never joined. You get motivated to make these important calls.

Monday, you are back in the office, all psyched up from the seminar. Three o'clock rolls around, and you stare at that telephone, knowing it's time to start. What do you do? You decide to drive to the printer's or shop for supplies. By the end of the week, you realize you have not made a single call. You figure, "Hmmm. Maybe I need a time management course or to join NAPMA Squared." So you take your 10th time management course, though time management has nothing to do with it and stacking more boxes on your desk or shelves will certainly not change the outcome. The problem is the control factor.

Think about where you came from and where you are now. You have your school. People respect you. People bow to you and refer to you with a respectful title like Master. If you make the telephone calls about joining your school, the distinct prospect is that someone will just say no, and you can't control that. So what do you do? Anything but make that call.

The control factor creates conflicting goals, and it paralyzes you. One positive goal that will improve your life is to grow your school, and making those calls is an important part of that growth. The other goal to have absolute control of your life prevents you from making those calls. Your goals conflict and cancel each other out.

Guess what? This happens to every one of us. It is the human experience. The key is to recognize it and then overcome the conflicting goals that are causing you to hesitate.

Remember, The Core Dynamics refer to the underlying forces that control the patterns of thought and behaviors that determine who we are. In this case, the underlying force, or Core Dynamic, is the *control factor*. How you handle the control factor is illustrated by your patterns of thought and behavior.

This is a key point. The most successful school owners have learned to manage the control factor and have overcome their conflicting goals. They realize and embrace the idea of short-term pain for long-term gain. The long-term gain of growing their school is a stronger goal that overcomes the short-tem pain of making the phone calls. The reverse is to take the short-term gain of not making the calls and suffer the long-term pain of a struggling school.

Protecting Your Puddle

The conflict that arises out of the control factor paralyzes most school owners. In a sense, they are now controlled by the control factor, which in truth puts him or her out of control (again). I call it protecting your puddle. I say puddle because that's as big as your school will get as long as it stays in the comfort zone of control. The owner has done a good job of using the martial arts to grow as a person but is now in a new arena and, instead of breaking through the conflicting goals to continue to grow, he or she hides inside a new box.

Many owners will avoid making those calls by checking their email 20 times or "networking" with another owner who is also avoiding making follow-up calls. The truth is that success only comes from action. While you are taking your 10th time management course, the successful owners are busy making those phone calls.

While you are doing what you can to avoid doing what you need to do, the successful owners are doing it. They are executing rather than planning or studying. Is studying important? Of course it is, but not during business hours or as an excuse to put off executing.

In the classic comic strip *Doonesbury*, the character Zonker Harris was a "professional student." He stayed in school as long as possible to avoid entering the real world. I am a lifelong student myself, but I also know it's easy to justify studying to avoid the real world of execution (here is a helpful rule: Spend at least five times as much time *doing* as *studying*).

The most successful school owners have learned to delegate, let go of control and try new ideas without fear of failure. They are not held back by their conflicting goals. They attack every day.

Where do Black Belt Eyes come from? For me, experiences like this. This is one of our inter-school tournaments circa 1975. The quality was as high as any state tournaments. Richard Jenkins of Texas is the referee. I'm sitting on the floor right behind him wondering if I'm going to get killed. I managed to win my junior brown belt fighting division.

The Truth About the
Martial Arts Business

Chapter Two
Finding Your Own Voice

In an advice column, a 15-year-old boy wrote, "I am 15, I have zits, my voice is still high, and no girl wants anything to do with me. What should I do?" The answer was really good.

It's not just you. Most 15-year-old boys are gawky and awkward and have zits. Girls your age are more interested in older boys. The question isn't what can you do now to improve your odds with girls, because there is really very little you can do now. The real question to focus on is: what kind of 18 year-old do you want to be? What can you do over the next three years to redefine yourself and create the person you think will have more success? Can you start lifting weights? Take martial arts and get a black belt? Get really good at some activity, other than video games or web surfing, so you have something going for you?

Many of us have experienced or observed a metamorphosis from the classic 98-pound weakling getting sand kicked in his face to a respected martial arts Master. Martial arts is truly a great way to redefine yourself.

By embracing the martial arts to the degree you and I did, we took major steps to redefine who we are and how we fit in the world. I thank the heavens for putting me in proximity to Walt Bone and Hank Farrah so that on February 12, 1974, I could take my first karate class.

I can't imagine what kind of life I would have led or what kind of person I would be had my life not taken that turn. I love being a black belt and a teacher. Even before training, I used to read biographies of all of my sports heroes. My goal was to become an athlete or a teacher. Martial arts provided me the opportunity to do both, and I am forever grateful. My goal now is to simply leave the martial arts in a better place than where I found it. That's a goal that motivates and rewards me daily.

When we learn from a specific instructor, it's natural for us to mimic somewhat his or her teaching methods, processes of control, and attitudes about teaching and the martial arts. Walt Bone taught me to teach through negative reinforcement. Never compliment a student. Always tell them what they are doing wrong. That's what I did for years. I became such an expert at pointing out things that could be improved upon that I did the same thing outside of school until a friend said I was hypercritical (you can see some of this negative teaching at www.martialartsteachers.com's *Truth About the Martial Arts Business* section).

The Square Block Lesson

When Mr. Bone said it was an unwritten rule that no one should open a school within five miles, I took that as the law. When Mr. Farrah explained that the purpose of the square block is to block one attacker in front of you with a modified side block and, at the same time, block another attacker from the side with a rising block, that is exactly what I believed.

That's how I taught the square block for almost two decades, until the day I was on a StairMaster® in a gym at the Cooper Institute, watching a karate class in front of me on the basketball court. The instructor was very good, and the 10 or so green belt adults were very attentive as he taught them the square block exactly as I was taught it and as I still taught it. But as I watched, I couldn't help but think: *that's the dumbest thing I've ever heard.* I wondered how any of us could keep a straight face while explaining this fantasy block.

Finding Your Own Voice is the process of questioning everything you teach, and all the systems within your school, to make sure they represent you and how you want to treat people. You want to make sure your program authentically reflects your beliefs... that it doesn't simply regurgitate what your instructor perpetuated on you. Just as an abused boy tends to become an abusive adult, abusive teaching practices, insane rituals, faulty reasoning, and myths can be passed on generation to generation until someone breaks the cycle and "finds his voice."

Finding Your Own Voice simply means you work to have a deeper understanding of the system, so that you don't keep explaining the square block as I did. You make the style serve your students, rather than the other way around. Just because your beloved instructor said it doesn't mean it's true. Just because some guy said it in the 1920s doesn't mean it's right for today. Don't strive to become a clone of your instructor or the masters in your system. Strive to be authentic as a person who uses martial arts as a way of expressing himself or herself.

The Truth About the Martial Arts Business

We Revere the Innovators of Change

Gichin Funakoshi, the father of Japanese karate, is renowned – and deservedly so – for making massive changes to Okinawan karate so it would be more acceptable to the Japanese. We have great systems like Shotokan today as a direct result of his efforts. But isn't changing a style to be accepted on a wider scale the ultimate in commercialization of the arts? Funakoshi had a deep understanding of the system, and he questioned everything. He made changes and found his own voice, and it's a voice that echoes throughout the martial arts world to this day.

Jigoro Kano stripped the deadly techniques from jujitsu and created judo. He founded Kodokan judo at age 22! He is also the creator of the colored belt system, which his friend Gichin Funakoshi adapted for karate. How would you respond today if a 22 year old told you he was changing your system and creating a new one? Most of us would think, who the heck are you to change this style?

Both of these martial arts heroes had the courage to question and innovate. Yet many of their descendants are passionate that the systems these men created should not change. It's as though the styles froze with the founders' passing.

Joe Lewis pays homage to his instructors, yet he has his own voice. He took his theories and ideas and battle-tested them in the ring and is still innovating to this day. In 30+ years of working with world-caliber martial artists, I have yet to see an instructor who even comes close to him. He lives, eats, and breathes martial arts.

Bill Wallace is a good friend of mine who is also very proud of his Okinawan roots, but he certainly has his own voice. Like Lewis, his voice is totally different than his instructors.

No unique voice in the martial arts has had the long-term impact of Bruce Lee. His instructor was Yip Man, but he was clear in his pursuit of truth in the martial arts and knew it could not be found in the confines of any style or label. Lee said that the martial arts are about honestly expressing yourself, and I totally agree. However, I don't see that a lot. I see a lot of robot-like mimicking and cloning. I see young instructors trying to call themselves Master, so they gain the implied wisdom that comes with that title.

Make Your School Authentically Yours

Finding Your Own Voice is the opposite. It's creating a school that authentically reflects you as a growing martial artist and as a human being, rather than quickly creating the illusion that you have already taken the journey and are on the other side as a Master. It's about surpassing your instructors in every way and being proud of it, rather than ashamed.

Today, in addition to the implied wisdom of positioning yourself like a Master Po from the *Kung Fu* TV series, we have the martial arts millionaire syndrome. Consultants present the image that they are martial arts millionaires and, if you do what they do, you can become one too. It can happen, but you want to make sure it's really the lifestyle you want.

I have a consulting client who has been very successful. He has one school, and it profits him $250,000 annually, but he wants four schools. Why? Because he took a martial arts business seminar, and the speaker said the way to wealth is multiple stores (yes, he even called them stores). My client has now opened another school and it is not only sucking him dry, but it is creating stress on his family.

I asked him why he got into teaching martial arts at all. He said he likes to help people and it's a good quality of life. Well, his quality of life has gone from good to bad quickly. He has lost touch with his original goals of teaching for a living. Even his big income is threatened, because he got excited about achieving someone else's goal. The seminar leader had goals of making millions, not quality of life. My client got caught up in it and allowed his own goals to be replaced by the seminar leader's goals. He found the seminar leader's voice, not his. This is a business example, but we often see a similar situation when a black belt remains in the shadow of his master for his entire career.

Where I Lost My Way

Know who you are, and why you are doing this. When I became a billing client of EFC, I attended one of their seminars in Atlanta. I was doing pretty good, but nothing like some of the EFC stars of the day. Still, it seemed the guys in Atlanta knew my name as a fighter, which was nice. As usual at these events, we shared information about student counts and, when I mentioned I had 245 students, they seemed impressed. They were even more impressed that my student body was mostly adults.

I didn't know there had been a huge boom in the children's market at the time due to *The Karate Kid*. The guys in Atlanta implied that I was missing half the market because I didn't have a lot of child students. I listened, thought about it, and then made one of my worse decisions as a school owner. I started doing the things they did to attract and keep kids. I started the student

**The Truth About the
Martial Arts Business**

creed, message of the week, and had kids screaming, "Yes, Sir!" on cue. In time, my school had totally changed from an adult school to a school full of kids or, as some like to call them, "a family school." Mind you, this was more the influence of EFC clients than EFC itself.

My income increased. I paid off my house and socked the money away, but I hated it. I didn't want to be at the school anymore. It was no fun explaining to a mom why her Miss Perfect daughter who gets straight As in school failed her blue belt exam. I had strayed big time from who I was as a martial artist and as a teacher.

Quality of life is a big issue with me and, for the first time in my martial arts career I had a job I didn't like. Most of the kids were fine, and many were great. But some kids just drove me nuts mostly because of the control factor. Controlling kids and their parents is not a fun way for a control freak to spend time. A lot of instructors like to teach kids, but I don't.

I had lost my way because I subscribed to someone else's vision. But I learned something important. Since then, I've tried to make it clear that you need to know yourself and what you want to do. This is especially true today, when so many programs are available.

Know What You Care About

I was the guy who created Cardio Karate in 1996, two years before the Tae Bo craze. I told the industry this was coming and that it was going to be big. But I never hid the fact that I would never teach a Cardio Karate class. I am a kickboxer, not a kick dancer. I have zero interest in kicking to an eight-beat. I created the Little Ninjas program characters with a Marvel Comics® artist. Great program, but I would never teach a Little Ninjas class or have the program in my school. I know who I am, and that is not for me.

When choosing from all the available programs, even mine, you have to be sure they reflect who you are and what you stand for. I still don't understand what an afterschool program has to do with martial arts. Not that it's a bad program. I see guys making lots of money with it, and that's great, but there is no way on earth I would do that.

I can't imagine a black belt dreaming about the perfect school: yeah, and then, after school, we'll have study hall and learn Spanish and tae kwon do. You may love teaching kids and helping them with their homework. That's great for you and for the kids. I just would never get excited about offering that program. Because I know my voice.

If you want to launch a program that reflects what you stand for, do it sooner than later.

You are going to make mistakes, so get them behind you quickly. This is a big step in dealing with the Control Factor. Double your failure rate by getting things going fast. Double your failure rate doesn't mean open and close twice as many schools. It means if you are not making mistakes you are not trying hard enough. If your heart is not in your throat at least once a day, you are taking it too safe. You have to try, trip, and get back up continually to get ahead.

Don't Let Setbacks Define You

Too many guys put off launching a Black Belt Club or Leadership Team because they are afraid it may not go well. Often it doesn't at first, but you get feedback and adjust it and keep going until you get it right. If you are in analysis paralysis, you will never launch the program. The adage about writing is that there is no writing, just rewriting. You will never get it perfect the first try, so make a mess and clean it up later. Just get on with it.

When a program doesn't go well, don't let the negative feedback define you. Know who you are, deeply and authentically. If I had let the setbacks I've encountered since 2003 define me, I wouldn't have launched MATA or be writing this book. Losing NAPMA doesn't make me a loser because setbacks or the actions of other people don't define me. I know who I am and what I am capable of. I'm an honest person, and I have confidence in my abilities. Sometimes the combination rubs people the wrong way, and I regret that. I never mean to offend anyone, but at least people can't say they don't know where they stand with me. They know.

Through this process I've learned that the only person I can control is myself. I have learned that I will conduct myself ethically, but I no longer have the expectation that anyone else will. Not to imply I'm the only ethical person in the industry – I deal with honest, upstanding people every day. But I agree with Donald Trump, a guy who has been through some messes. He said that if you expect the worst from someone, you won't get surprised. Although I'm not a negative person, the lawsuits and fallout have taught me much about this industry and myself.

I always try to turn a negative into a positive, and I have, with MATA and this book. My attitude and spirit have been tested, and I've held up well. It's easy to be positive when everything is going well. But pressure uncovers your true beliefs. Pressure exposes people, and I am happy with the way I've handled these setbacks. I found I have not been simply spewing positive attitude platitudes all these years. I discovered the power of resilient optimism. I really believe that good things happen if you stay the course and remain confident in your abilities.

Here are some instances in my own life where I was challenged by circumstances beyond my control. In each case, I turned the negative situation into a positive outcome:

Negative Action	Positive Reaction
Parents wouldn't pay for karate	Clean school for lessons
Get laid off from teaching	Open community center class
Instructor dies in plane crash	Assume his college class
Fired from college	Open USA Karate
Going broke	Travel and study successful schools
	Write *Black Belt Management* which leads to me creating NAPMA
Lose NAPMA/MAPro	Launch Martial Arts Teachers' Association
	Write *The Truth About the Martial Arts Business*

The Characters

This chapter has been about Finding Your Own Voice. Let me wrap it up with some typical martial artist characters. When you meet these guys you'll know they have not yet found their own voice.

The Tough Guy

Once I saw the Tough Guy as a corner judge in a point match. He refused to move. When a fighter complained, this guy threatened to "pound him." Martial arts has not made these guys better people, as much as it has given them additional weapons to bully and intimidate. They need to be extra tough and aggressive to make sure no one thinks they aren't. This is someone my grandmother would call a very small man.

Travis Bickle

Travis is the character played by Robert DeNiro in *Taxi Driver*. Bickle doesn't do martial arts per se but transforms himself into a militant vigilante. His was the classic scene in front of the mirror as he pretends to confront someone with the line, "You talkin' to me? You talkin' to me? Then, who you talkin' to?"

In high school, I wore karate pants, my karate school T-shirt, and wooden Japanese sandals. I was like Travis in adopting a new identity. I was "Karate Jock." I grew out of it. Some guys never do.

Typically, these people are more fringe martial artists than hard core. They play-act like they are martial artists more than they actually engage in structured training. I knew one who seemed to learn everything from books. Somehow he got a black belt and taught students in his garage. His living room was a weight gym/dojo. Travis Bickles are fascinated by the martial arts but never seem to undergo extended training under one instructor or system. Mind you, that won't stop them from getting a black belt.

At best, they are lifelong dabblers in the martial arts. At the worst, well, they may not be far off from Travis Bickle.

Mr. Negative

Mr. Negative has seen everything and tried everything, but nothing works for his school. He blames his area, his economy, the belt factory down the street, or the current president for his school's struggles. He is critical of everyone and everybody. He starts sentences with, "The problem with _____ is . . ." Insert a name, style, system, idea, tournament, or business idea in the blank, and you have Mr. Negative. Not a fun guy.

Crusty the Clown

With the movement toward personal development in the classroom, some instructors work hard to look like perfect role models. They talk like a rehashed motivational speaker: "What are you passionate about now?" They try to come off as a hybrid Mr. Rogers and Robin Williams. Truthfully, they remind me more of a character from *The Simpsons* named Crusty the Clown. Crusty is a favorite of the kids, who idolize him and watch every episode of his children's TV show. But as soon as the camera is off, he pops a beer, lights a cigarette, and starts complaining about the kids. Watch out for Crusty the Clowns wearing black belts and making you laugh. Hold onto your wallet, and hide your female students.

The Enlightened One

Did you ever speak with a high ranking black belt who seemed to turn everything you say into a metaphor for nature or world peace? He doesn't speak as much as give speeches.

Master Po

I know a guy who makes his wife call him Master. Another man calls himself Grand Master. That's nothing new, but one day his non-martial arts wife said, "All these people call you Grand Master, what title can I have?" Not exactly what I'd call an authentic person.

The Retro-Warrior

Every conversation ends up a war story from the blood-and-guts days. This guy's dream is for it to be 1975 again. When the only thing you have going for you currently is an event that happened decades ago, you have stopped trying. The Retro-Warrior peaked a long time ago and does his best to relive those times year after year, even as his school crumbles around him. These guys are fun to spend time with because they often have great stories. In fact, this reminds me of the time I was fighting in London and...

The Asian Wannabe

This is the freakiest of all martial arts characters. This is a Caucasian who is so enamored of the Asian roots of the martial arts and, even more so, of his Asian master that he actually begins to speak with an Asian accent. Some people call it pigeon talk. I call it weird.

The Martial Arts Millionaire

Conversations with this guy start as an interrogation about how many students you have and what you are grossing and end as a bragging session all about money, money, money. Boring, boring, boring. If I ever do this to you, you have my permission to choke me out.

Joe Lewis (l) moved in with Mr. Bone (r) in 1977 for about six-months. The first night he was there, Lewis lined up the brown and black belts and fought each one of us. I remember he hit me with a backfist, then told the class he hit me in the forehead so it wouldn't hurt.

I was thinking, "Oh Man! He's picking parts of my face to hit..."

The top shot is Lewis teaching class with Mr. Bone. The bottom shot is from his seminar on Clearwater Beach in 1977.

The Truth About the Martial Arts Business

Chapter Three
Value What You Do

One time I had a guy come into my school with one of my flyers. The offer was three months and a uniform for $249. He said he stopped by another school by mistake. When he presented the flyer to the school's owner, his comment was, "I can tell you one thing: he's charging you too much."

This guy was 10 years my senior and had made his living as a martial arts school owner for much longer than I had. Yet I had three times as many students at twice the tuition. He was a 10th degree black belt, and I was just a third or fourth at the time. What did he mean when he said I was charging too much? What is too much? Why did he place less value on martial arts than I did?

If I could pay you $10,000, would you sell me your black belt? Would you strip martial arts from your life for 10 grand, as though you never took that first class? How about 20? Deal? I didn't think so. I've never met a black belt who would. If you could take a new student forward in time to give him or her the feeling of being a black belt, do you think they would miss classes? Do you think they would hesitate to join your school at twice the price you are currently charging? How are you reflecting that value in your school?

In a Western society, quality is always associated with higher price. I'm not just trying to get you to raise your prices; I really don't care what you charge. But I do care that you recognize and Value What You Do. That sense of value is reflected in a number of ways, including tuition. In more than a decade of consulting with school owners, I find this is the Core Dynamic that stifles them the most. This is the most common problem for school owners.

This is an especially important message for those of you teaching a traditional system. Many traditionalists place a high value on what they teach, but they don't demonstrate or reflect that value. Their school is kind of ratty, the systems on how to enroll are unclear, and the efforts to create and keep students are haphazard at best. They may speak of the value of martial arts, but they don't demonstrate it.

This could apply to any school, but traditionalists have taken the noble path of preserving our core martial arts styles. In order for that to happen– and I certainly hope it does – the value of what martial arts represent has to be reflected in every element of the school.

At the core of Value What You Do is this attitude:

I am a highly skilled, unique professional in our community. There are very few, if any, people who can provide the service and benefits that I can. I am not going to spend my time, stress, and money teaching people who are not committed to earning a black belt with me.

If your response is, "That would never work in my area," then the Core Dynamic of Value What You Do is exactly the issue for you to focus on. Again, this is the most common problem with martial arts schools.

Even though we have personally undergone an amazing transformation through the martial arts, and we speak about the high value of martial arts, many of us do not demonstrate it in how we run our business. This is not about tuition. This is about every aspect of your school, from logo design to black belt graduations.

Ask your local private school about the enrollment process. I guarantee you they have a specific step-by-step process to qualify the student and then enroll him or her. You can be sure they have a contract and that a child will fail for underperformance. However, the school has few failures, because they have a system to get students ready to pass.

When you have a clear, consistent process to enroll students and qualify them for black belt, you show them that you Value What You Do. If you fear setting your prices more than $10 higher than the competition, you do not Value What You Do. Price, contracts, or using a billing company are not deciding factors for joining a school.

If your enrollment process is to let whoever answers the phone do her best – without consistent training – to get the prospect to come in, you don't Value What You Do. Like the private school – you show prospects the value of what you do by making sure the system for answering the phone and setting appointments is clear and consistently booking 8 out of every 10 phone calls into good appointments.

If your enrollment process is to teach an intro or just let them join the class, without a proven system for moving a prospect from stranger to student 8 out of 10 times, you don't Value What You Do. You demonstrate to your prospects that you Value What You Do by having a trial lesson program that is well thought out and rehearsed so that 8 out of 10 students who take it enroll.

If you advertise that you are a month-to-month school and that students can cancel anytime, you don't Value What You Do. You Value What You Do when you adopt the attitude that you are a skilled professional, and you will not pour your heart into teaching someone who is only going to drop out when football season starts.

Here is the truth. In every market, the school that sets the highest tuition and uses contracts and has a professional system from the logo to the black belt exam and beyond has the most students. Everything about their operation demonstrates that they place a high value on what they do. Smaller schools that offer no contracts and lower tuition usually surround the high-value schools, yet they struggle.

These Things Demonstrate That You Value What You Do:

1. Your Black Belt Club is only for students who have committed to earn their black belt.
2. Your black belt exam process includes extra classes and opportunities to train for black belt candidates.
3. You have a professionally designed logo and marketing materials.
4. You indoctrinate the student from day one on the value of earning a black belt.
5. You keep a very clean school and replace worn equipment.
6. You have systems for every aspect of your school.
7. You use agreements instead of a month-to-month option.
8. You fail students who do not perform to the standards of the rank.
9. You study and train like a student for life.
10. You realize you can't be the best and the cheapest, so you commit to being the best.

The most successful school owners highly value what they do... and it shows in every aspect of their school.

As a new karate student in 1974, this was my first school event. We
tore down a two-story house with punches and kicks.
It took all day to finish the job.

I'd heard of breaking boards and bricks but breaking a house?
This had to be a great school!

As you can imagine, there were a lot of injuries, but that just
reinforced the need to be tough

That is the "Suntan Superman" Hank Farrah surveying the damage.

The Truth About the
Martial Arts Business

Chapter Four
Clarity of Purpose

The martial arts are much like show business. There is confusion and internal conflict about money. "Serious" artists are concerned that they not sell out or become commercial. I saw a martial arts "master" on an A&E special. He said, "Martial arts is about changing lives. It's not about making money." This is classic, "Master Po" in action.

That kind of easy-to-spew rhetoric creates confusion. The history of martial arts is rife with stories of "masters" teaching the arts altruistically. When you hear one of those stories, it's usually from someone who thinks charging for martial arts is wrong. Just keep in mind that:

There is a big difference between you and the story teller or the kind master – they don't have to pay your bills. You do!

Like sex, money is seldom discussed, other than to complain about the lack of it. If you were raised in a family that struggled financially, you may have certain beliefs drilled into your head: such as, "The rich get richer, while the poor get poorer." "We can't afford that!" "I'd rather be happy than rich." "Money is the root of all evil." "The rich put their pants on one leg at a time." Or, my favorite of all time, "If money was so important, look at who God gave it to."

The message is that not only will you not have money but also that people who have money have sold their soul. The truth is that money is like a hammer: it's just a tool. Money is also blind; it doesn't care who has it or uses it. If you save your money, your wealth grows. If you spend it, your wealth shrinks. Money doesn't care one way or the other.

When you combine that kind of negative association with money – which is very common, by the way – and throw in the effusive spiritual underpinnings of the martial arts, you get idiotic statements like the one from the Master Po guy on A & E.

Because the martial arts can be a power for good, many of us convince ourselves that we teach to help people. We feel we should sacrifice our own well-being to "help the children." We charge too little, and we let people train for free and, when they get good enough, we hire them to teach. When they underperform we keep them on, because, well, Sally has been with me for six years. If I fire her, I don't know what she would do.

Many of us worked hard to make all our students happy, and I don't mean only from a student service standpoint. Our reward is that smile on little Johnny's face, or Cindy's improved grades, or Joe's raise at work because we gave him the confidence to ask for it. Most professions don't offer those rewards. In fact, that is all the reward we need, right? Wrong. Very, very wrong. Beware this dangerous trap of rationalization.

When your well-being depends on how happy your students are, doctors call that co-dependency, and it will eat you alive. There is no way you can keep all of your students, much less keep them all happy. This approach will wear you down and burn you out, because the human experience is a balance of good and bad for all of us, including our students.

You Must Take Care of Yourself First

I have learned that you can't honestly give yourself to anyone unless your needs are met first. Initially it sounds selfish, but it's a healthy kind of selfishness. In the safety briefing before a flight, the attendant reminds you to fasten your own oxygen mask before you help someone else. You will be in a much better position to help people in your school if you are grossing $30,000 per month, because you are taking care of yourself first, rather than grossing $10,000 because you are "helping the children."

The Risk is High So Take the Reward

The reason you sign the lease, risk your money, risk lawsuits, risk losing everything is not to help the children. The reason is to build wealth for your family.

This is a key mindset, and the top school owners are crystal clear on it.

The purpose of your school is to build wealth for your family. You accomplish this by becoming the best teacher in your town and having a strong business system to support your teaching, so that you can reach and help more people. You create wealth by helping people.

Imagine you are the owner of a television network. You don't take a risk like that just to have shows that will help the children. You offer some educational programs in the public interest and others that are pure entertainment. But you bought the network to create wealth for your family. You do that by hiring the best talent, equipment, and programming possible.

This is especially true when you have a family. It's simply not fair to drag your spouse and children through the life of a martial artist if you are not going to build a future for them.

The purpose of your school is to send *your* kids to good schools, to provide *your* spouse with a feeling of security and certainty that things are going to be OK financially and to give *you* the opportunity to retire in dignity. You accomplish this by being the best school owner and instructor in your town. Once you adopt this attitude, business becomes less stressful, because it's easier to make decisions when you have Clarity of Purpose.

Chase your passion but, don't chase away profits or your families' future doing so.

This is How I Earn My Income

As Abraham Lincoln put it, "We can't help the poor by becoming one of them." I heard one of my mentors, a plastic surgeon, speak on the phone with a patient who asked for a discount or payment terms. He said, "Miss, this is how I earn my income. You can make payments and, when they are all done, we can do the surgery; otherwise, we're going to have to wait until you can afford it." That is Clarity of Purpose. Plastic surgery, like martial arts, is a choice.

Western society will never take martial arts seriously as a business, activity, or potential career if we all live hand to mouth. How can you teach the success life skills so popular today if you have never experienced success as a teacher? Would you want someone to teach you how to run a martial arts school who has never even owned a business, much less a martial arts school? I hope not.

Cardinal Rule – *Never sacrifice the needs of your family for your students.*

The most successful school owners are crystal clear that the purpose of their school is to build wealth for their families. Create profit – not poverty – from your passion.

Our famed Friday Night Black Belt Workouts featured two hours of forms, fighting, and fun. These were very loose but really intense workouts. The Friday Night Black Belt Workout was the ultimate "inner-circle in our school. You worked hard and dreamed of the day you could get the heck pounded out of you on Friday night as part of this group.

The guy in the lacross helmet is Walt Bone. His nose had been broken 11 times, so he wore the helmet to protect it. Bone's dog was always chasing our ankles as we sparred.

The Truth About the
Martial Arts Business

Chapter Five
Black Belt Eyes

In the early months of NAPMA, my art director Scott Kelby and I created a black-and-white ad of a student throwing a nice jump side kick under a great headline, "Kids Don't Seem to Mind Our Summer School." The ad was a big hit. Schools reported 40 to 60 phone calls, more than they had ever received. Some members, though, wanted to cancel because they didn't do that technique. Others complained because they wore white uniforms, but the kid in the ad was in a black and grey gi. This is a classic example of Black Belt Eyes.

Black Belt Eyes are when we assume someone sees, understands and feels the same way about an aspect of the martial arts as we do.

Black Belt Eyes are natural and good. I have them to this day. It's just important that we are aware of when they might be getting in the way of what we are trying to accomplish, which is to attract and keep students.

Black Belt Eyes illustrate how the Core Dynamics are reflected in what we do. In most cases, Black Belt Eyes are based upon false assumptions. For instance, with the jump side kick ad, the guys who canceled may have feared that a mom would bring the ad in and say, "I want to enroll my child, but first show me this kick." Or, "Do you have that uniform in white, like this ad?" Of course, that never happens, but we are so deeply connected to our systems that our Black Belt Eyes often get in the way of our more useful *Market Eyes*. Black Belt Eyes assumed people would see they wore a different color uniform or wouldn't recognize the technique. Market Eyes are the eyes of your potential students, who don't know a jump side kick from a jumping jack.

We Know Too Much

When Black Belt Eyes see an ad with a jump side kick, they are drawn to the most important aspect of the ad for black belts. It's not the headline, the copy, or the offer. Black Belt Eyes will check to make sure the kid has his foot bladed and the other foot is tucked. That's not a bad thing. It reflects your standards as a black belt. But if you choose not to run that ad because you don't do jump kicks, then your Black Belt Eyes may have cost you 40 to 60 phone calls which should have converted to 20 to 30 new students.

Black Belt Eyes work against you when you assume that a person with little or no martial arts experience will feel the same about it as you do.

A Black Belt Eyes ad will have someone getting kicked in the head. The owner knows that one of life's simple pleasures is wrapping your foot around someone's head with a hook or round kick. The readers, however, with their Market Eyes, may translate that image into what will happen to them at that school. They can't even imagine getting their leg up that high, so they are not identifying with the kicker.

Black Belt Eyes tell the market what it needs instead of listening to the market and giving it what it wants. Black Belt Eyes show that we care about what we do. They are not bad, but you have to be aware of them. Most of all, recognize when they get in your way.

Has a spouse or significant other made a suggestion about your school or how you teach? What was your reaction? I know mine was essentially 'Who the heck are you to tell me, the black belt, about martial arts?' The key, though, is:

> They don't care about martial arts; they care about you.
> They usually represent Market Eyes, and they are almost always right.

Other examples of Black Belt Eyes include:

1. Using your style name as a headline or, worse, a school name.
This is a huge assumption that the reader or prospect knows how your style or technique translates to benefits for them.

2. Using a logo that looks like martial arts hieroglyphics.

If your logo contains a fist, a yin-yang, a circle, a triangle, Asian lettering, or a bug, you may have Black Belt Eyes. As quickly as you can, seek professional help with the MATA Logo Design service at www.martialartsteachers.com.

3. Listing techniques instead of benefits in your marketing.

This may disappoint you, but the odds are miniscule that someone seeing an ad that touts Hun Gar 3 Step Waza will exclaim to his wife, "Honey! Hun Gar 3 Step Waza! Just what I've always wanted!" Only your Black Belt Eyes will know what that means. I don't even know what it means.

4. Confusing your wins as benefits.

Black Belt Eyes assume people want to know that you are an accomplished black belt. It's not that no one cares, as much as that listing your tournament wins, hall of fame inductions, or that you trained the military police simply don't translate into benefits for potential students. Mike Tyson is a great boxer, but I don't want him teaching my kids. Study the ads for private schools. They don't list the teachers' résumés. Market Eyes want to know what you can do for them or their children.

5. Having long classes.

The assumption is that more is better. The truth is that better is better. If more were better, a four-hour class would be better than a two-hour class. People are busy, and it's presumptuous to assume that your class is so important it has to take two hours of their day. Most people have 16 waking hours per day. Two hours is more than 10 percent of that day. Good instructors can teach a great class and produce outstanding black belts using one-hour classes. If your classes are longer than this, reduce them to one hour. Your students will not complain. They will thank you.

6. Keeping archaic exam requirements that are important to you, not the student.

When I was a student, for part of your brown belt exam you had to break two boards with a reverse punch, round kick two boards, and do a running jump side kick over two people to break three boards. This was for the blue belt to fourth degree (kyu or kup) brown belt and usually occurred about a year into training. I opened my school with the same requirements. I have great video of my black belts like Kathy Marlor breaking and bouncing off boards during these marathon exams.

When the children's invasion began in the mid-1980s, those requirements became a real problem. Eight- and 10 year olds have no business doing those types of breaks. So I dropped board breaking as a requirement and added board-breaking seminars that the students could pay to attend. I turned a negative element of the belt exam process into a fun profit center. To accomplish this, I had to overcome my Black Belt Eyes (you can see video of some of those exams in the *Truth About the Martial Arts Business* section of www.martialartsteachers.com).

7. Conducting marathon exams.

During the days of my marathon Saturday exams, it seemed as though we measured the quality of an exam by the number of ambulance calls. I thought it was important for students to deal with the stress of the high-pressure, marathon exams because it would help them deal with the stress of self defense, which is just dumb. I also waited until enough people were ready before I held the exam. This is classic Black Belt Eyes combined with the Control Factor.
In time, I switched to monthly exams (stripes and belts) that were held in class. This greatly increased retention and student progress – and reduced stress.

8. Displaying weapons on the wall or in the office.

You may love weapons but, to the market, a wall full of knives, swords, and spears looks like a weapons cache. Mothers in particular do not respond well to the prospects of their darling child being exposed to these instruments of death.

9. Displaying photos of yourself hitting, getting hit, or breaking.

One school had a photo of the instructor being front kicked, full power, in the groin. His Black Belt Eyes felt that the photo showed he could withstand any blow. My Market Eyes made me wince and turn away. There is nothing interesting, appealing, or tasteful about such a photo. Take down the 1989 photos of you and replace them with pictures of your happy students. It's OK to have a shot of yourself; just make sure it's tasteful and professionally shot. Media coverage, such as magazine covers or newspaper articles, are also fine. Tip: If you are on a TV show, have someone take a photo that includes the cameras. This is a good way to get mileage out of a TV appearance. You can't post a video on your wall, but this type of photo shows you were on a TV show. Media appearances build confidence in students and prospects. Photos of you breaking flaming bricks don't.

10. Having a smelly school.

This could be called Black Belt Nose. When prospects walked into my school, their eyes watered and their faces contorted from the sweaty stench soaked into our carpet. I used to tell them with pride, "We earned that smell . . ." Not good.

11. Sparring too soon.

Black Belt Eyes say, "Sparring prepares you for self defense." Market Eyes say, "That's scary, and it hurts." Few things lead to high dropouts faster than sparring. Sparring is important, and I love it. But the smartest curriculum adjustment I ever made was to push back the time when students had to spar. Rather than after three months, which was how I was raised, it became eight months. During those eight months, we work on limited sparring drills and defense and prepare the students how to spar before they are thrown in the ring.

I made the change after years of having the following scenario played out too often. Typically, a female student would enroll and soon become an A student. She was in every class. She was at every function. She volunteered to help. She changed her work hours or made changes in her life to make sure she could do karate.

This lasted for three months until she reached the rank where sparring was required. Then I wouldn't see her again until I ran into her at the mall or a restaurant. You say, "Sally! Nice to see you. We sure miss you in class." She says, "Oh, um, hi, Mr. Graden. I've been really busy lately. Gotta go."

If I had a Truth Translator, the real message would be, "I trusted you. I really trusted you and embraced your school into my life. Then you put me up against that guy, and I had no idea what to do. He hit me on my nose, and it hurt. I will not trust you again." When I tell this story in seminars, the classic Black Belt Eyes vs Market Eyes exchange reveals itself, as the owners' wives and girlfriends elbow them in the ribs. "I told you!"

Some guys argue that sparring is important. I agree. However, how can you teach sparring to someone who drops out?

Today, people – especially women – are taught never to hit someone. We have to be patient and help them get comfortable with the idea of hitting and getting hit. We have to give them strategies to get out of the way of a bigger, faster opponent and, most of all, we have to drill them over and over so they are ready to spar when they reach that level.

12. Setting heavy traditional requirements in the first year.

If your white belt class consists of traditional stances, blocks, and forms, you are going to have a tough time keeping students. Try to make sure your white belt material gives your student *Instant Value*. Give your students material they can use right away.

We pushed all of our traditional tae kwon do techniques back to green belt. White, gold, and orange belt were spent on working on pad drills, practical self defense, sparring, and footwork drills. The students loved it. They felt a sense of competence right away. As important as they are, the traditional martial arts are very hard to learn. By front-loading your curriculum with your core traditional material, you put some of the most difficult techniques to learn with your most inexperienced students.

This is especially true for children. Forms were created by highly disciplined adults to be taught to other highly disciplined adults. They were not designed to be taught to eight-year-old kids with ADHD.

Teaching a new student a front stance and then trying to layer on a down block-lunge punch is not only hard, but you almost have to apologize for the lack of practicality. We say things like, "You would never really block this way, but this is a block against a kick to the groin." That, my friend, is Black Belt Eyes in action.

13. Having too many "shoulds" in your curriculum.

It's natural for a new school owner to have dreams of creating a great martial arts school. He dreams that his black belts will be the best, and people will flock to his school. When this enterprising black belt sits down to design the ultimate curriculum, he thinks to himself, "Hmmm. My students *should* learn the traditional basics. They *should* be able to do a form or two each belt. They *should* know the basic traditional stances and blocks. They *should* be able to do all the kicks and punches. They *should* learn some self defense. They *should* be able to do one-steps and spar as well."

There are two consequences to this line of thinking.

1. Each requirement will have to be covered in class to prepare students for their exams.
2. With so many requirements, students will have less time to work on each, so quality will be difficult to obtain and maintain.

When you have too many requirements for each belt, you are strapping yourself to covering those techniques in each class. If you don't cover them, students will not be ready for exams, and it won't be their fault. If you have 20 requirements for an orange belt exam, you have to spend a large amount of class covering these 20 techniques. With that many requirements being covered each class, your creativity is hindered. Your classes will tend to be the same. This level of repetition is good only to the degree you don't lose students to boredom.

The key is to require only the base skills on exams. You'll have to decide what those base skills are. You can still teach the other 100 techniques you think students "should" learn, but you don't box yourself in as a teacher. For instance, I can teach a spin hook kick to a class of blue belts but not require it on an exam. It's not a core technique, but it is fun.

Self-defense escapes can also fall into this category, though it depends. Self defense is at the core of most programs but, typically, it's not taught very well, and it's hard to practice. There is a lot of speculation, "I do this, which will make him do that . . ." in self defense that is style based. Realistically, a headlock escape practiced at 50 percent speed and power works 100 percent of the time. A headlock escape practiced at 75 percent speed and power works less. But how well does it work when both students are going at it 100 percent? Most of us never do that, so who knows?

Students have a finite amount of time to practice your curriculum. If they have 20 techniques to master in order to pass your orange belt exam, they will spend half the amount of time on each technique than if they only had 10 techniques. For example, in a 12-week testing cycle you expect students to attend class twice a week. This is a total of 24 hours in class. In each class, you devote 20 minutes to requirements. That is a total of eight hours working on test requirements. Some requirements, like forms, take much more time to master, while others, like a ridge hand, take less time.

It only makes sense that a student who has 10 requirements to learn in eight hours will spend twice as much time on each one as a student who has 20 to learn. Conversely, an instructor will have twice as much time on each of 10 requirements in eight hours than one who has to cover 20. Odds are, the students with 10 requirements will have a higher competence level than those with 20.

Our Black Belt Eyes lead us to believe that our students will be good because they know more, but again, more is not better. Better is better. Fewer requirements make better students and aid retention, because students who feel they are doing well are happy students and stay in the school. Competence leads to confidence.

Just remember that Market Eyes pay the bills. The next time your spouse or significant other makes the suggestion that tying students together with a belt and having them spar may not be a good move, take a deep breath, listen, and say, "Thank you. Good point."

Your life is defined by your patterns of behavior and thought. Actions do speak louder than words. The Core Dynamics are five crucial areas of our professional life. The top school owners manage the Control Factor; they have Found Their Own Voice; they Value What They Do; they have Clarity of Purpose; and they balance their Black Belt Eyes with educated Market Eyes.

One of the many media interviews I did while teaching at St. Petersburg Junior College in Florida. I had a great experience teaching there from about 1982 to 1985. This came to and end when the Students for Christ successfully petitioned the school to discontinue Eastern Humanities, Yoga, and Karate.

I had taken over the class after Mr. Bone died. When the class was discontinued, I began teaching at a local community center.

Just like today, regardless of the situation, I always find a place to teach.

**The Truth About the
Martial Arts Business**

Section Two
What Works

Bruce Lee was the first well-known advocate of the "use what works and discard the rest" attitude towards training. While no one has inspired more people in the martial arts than Bruce, Joe Lewis had more direct influence on the application of fighting techniques, strategies ,and tactics simply because he battle-tested everything. He used his own fights and experience as laboratories to discover what was truth and what was theory.

This title of this book is *The Truth About the Martial Arts Business*. In homage to these legends, this section is called What Works. For 20- years, I taught martial arts as a profession. I earned a six-figure income and produced one world champion and many excellent black belts, some of whom are in positions of influence within the industry. Kathy Marlor (MartialCoach. com), Rob Colasanti, and Kevin Walker of Project Action were my students from white belt up. I'm very proud of my track record as a teacher and the continuing contributions my students make to this industry.

After selling my schools and launching NAPMA, I spent the next 10 years seeking out and working with the most successful martial arts school owners in North America. Now, with the Martial Arts Teachers' Association, my classroom is global and so are the information resources I'm able to use to find out what really works in today's market.

This section has no theory, myths or pretense. Quite simply, here is what has proven to work regardless of location, style or the state of the economy. As we discovered in The Core Dynamics, it's what you think about and then execute that will make the difference.

Anyone can make excuses. Only you can make progress.

My humble beginnings after losing the college job: teaching the only white belt
to show up at my new community center class.

I was never discouraged though. I was always happy that I could
actually be paid to teach and work in my bare feet and gi.

**The Truth About the
Martial Arts Business**

Chapter Six
Positioning Your School for Success

A rule of design that most guys don't know is that, when you hang a picture, you want the picture to complement the frame and the frame to complement the room. Though this chapter is not about school design, this example illustrates the three elements that must work together to make a picture work. The three parallel dynamics that must work together for a martial arts school to have a chance in any location are the area, the rent, and the space.

If you are in the wrong area or in the wrong part of a good area, you will not generate the traffic you need regardless of your space. If you are paying way too much rent, you will start each month scrambling to survive the next one. This kills cash flow. Your goal with rent is always to keep it under 15% of your gross. A good rule of thumb is that your average gross is ten times your rent. So, for a $4,000 rent to work, you want to gross $40,000 or more.

Too often, new owners build their school as the over-large and over-built Fantasy School they've always dreamed of. This is a classic case of Black Belt Eyes. We are building the school for our black belt buddies and ourselves, instead of our target market.

The Area

The area you choose for your school must match the market you want to reach. There is a big difference between the most appropriate areas for an adult kickboxing school, a kids' school, and a school that caters to wealthy executives. The kickboxing school would do best surrounded by condos and apartments. The kids' school wants to be triangulated by public schools in single-family home neighborhoods. The guy teaching wealthy executives might need only a room in a health club in the downtown business district, provided there are enough potential executives to support the idea.

Let's look at some markets and what kind of school best matches that market. Keep in mind that there are exceptions to every rule, and these are general rules of thumb.

The Small Town

Small towns are about 50,000 in population or less. If you are good at developing a name, it's much easier to do so in a smaller town like these than in larger, more competitive areas. In some rural areas, there is not as much for kids, families, and adults to do as in larger cities, so your school can become a recreational and social center of the town.

Also, schools in smaller towns don't have much competition. There may be a class at the YMCA or a part-time school, but often these are run like hobbies by black belts who enjoy teaching but have no immediate prospect as a full-time professional.

Some areas, like the town where I live in Florida, are small towns as defined here, but they are surrounded by more densely populated small cities, which expand the potential market considerably. In these areas, the rent is usually affordable – even in more affluent towns, which is great news for your cash flow. Cost of living tends to be significantly less too, so you can live comfortably on far less. In fact, in comparison to large cities, what might buy you a high standard of living in a small town might not even get you a small apartment in a large city.

The Small City

The city with a 50,000-100,000 population range is a sweet spot for many schools. These areas can be gold mines for a well-positioned school. These are often predominately middle-income areas with pockets of high and low income. Because they share many of the advantages of the smaller town, it's easier to build your name and less expensive to market to, and rents are lower than those in the bigger cities. Also, because the area is larger, you will have more potential locations from which to choose.

The Medium City

The city with a 100,000-250,000 population may be more expensive and not as easy to penetrate as the smaller markets. But the increased population density and the larger number of potential locations make these great markets for an organized school. Competition will be more plentiful but, odds are, if you are a MATA member, you will have what it takes to be top dog within a couple of years. Even if you don't make it to number one, there is plenty of business to go around.

My school in St. Petersburg, Florida, was a perfect example of this market. I was able to secure a 2,500-square-foot space in a remote corner of a plaza for about $1,000 per month when I opened my first school. Once I got over my Fantasy School period and learned how to run a school, we were generating $20,000-$30,000 per month, and we opened a second location in town a few years later.

The Large City

To paraphrase the song, "If you can make it there, you'll make it anywhere...." Large cities have their own set of advantages and disadvantages. Competition will be stiff and rent high. If you can find the right space at the right rent, and you are a good teacher with a strong business system, the high population density can work as an advantage to get you profitable.

The biggest I've seen is the Tiger Shulmann school in downtown Manhattan. It is a 20,000-square-foot prime location with three training floors and a café. Neither Billy Blanks' school in Ventura, California nor the main Krav Maga school in Los Angeles, California, are nearly as big as Tiger's, but both have great locations and are packed with students. Billy has to have a valet parking system because he is busy all day. A couple of years ago, I took a Tae Bo class there at 10 a.m. with 67 other people, mostly women. The class after ours was taught by Billy and had more than 100 students lined up for it. This was all before lunch!

I use these examples not to imply that you have to have a location and school like any of them. I just want you to know what the highest level of competition is in the biggest metro areas in the USA, Los Angeles and New York City.

Potential Ratio

Your potential ratio is the percentage of the population that has a realistic potential of joining your school. The number used for decades has been 1.5%. Due to the explosion of exposure and credibility the martial arts gained from the fitness kickboxing boom in the mid-1990s, I personally feel the number is larger than that. But, to be safe, let's say two percent of the population may join your school. This applies mostly to medium and larger cities and metro areas as defined above. Smaller cities and towns can draw a much higher percentage of the population, depending on the demographics and the type of program being offered.

Let's say you are in a 100,000-population area, which means you have a potential ratio of 2,000 students. Sounds great, right? Well, slow down. First, those 2,000 are the potential for all of the martial arts classes combined. Your job, of course, is to get more than your competitors. Second, what if they live on the other side of town?

Pull Radius

Your pull radius is the area surrounding your school, from which your students will come. Typically, a student will not drive more than 10-15 minutes to your school. Yes, yes, yes, I know you have students who drive an hour and walk uphill both ways to get to your classes, but unless you are going to charge those three people $1,000 per class, you can't build a school around them.

The real question is, how much of my potential ratio is within my pull radius? Here is just a sample of the factors that will influence the answer:

1. Regardless of the population of your area, what is the population within your pull radius? Multiply that by .02 to get your potential ratio.

2. Is your school near a natural barrier? Where I live, there is a subtle bridge north of us. While there is nothing stopping us from crossing it, we rarely do. We turn south on the main roads to travel to shops, restaurants, and parks. I'm sure there are good restaurants and shops across the bridge, but we don't go there, and I'm sure people on the other side don't come south to our area. Other barriers include railroad tracks, rivers, bridges, busy highways, and tunnels.

3. What are the real demographics of your pull radius? Do you have the area's largest trailer park or retired person's community inside your pull radius? You're not going to get two percent of those markets.

The demographics within your pull radius will make you or break you. Your job is to match your pull-radius demographic with your school.

Demographics

For our purposes, we will narrow your demographic focus to those people within your pull radius. Imagine setting a ring with the radius of a 15-minute drive on a map of your area and then moving it around. Wherever you move the ring the demographics will change. Our goal is to find the best demographics within that ring. Keep in mind that a 15-minute drive ring will be much smaller for a densely populated area with lots of traffic than a more rural area. A 15 minute drive in Orlando or London could be two miles, while it could be 15 miles or more in smaller, less congested areas, so be realistic in your ring size. You have to know the size of your pull radius.

Once you zero in on a location, drive from the location at different times that your students would be going to class, so you can experience and time the drive, to see how far you get in 15-minutes.

If two percent of your ring is your potential ratio, a population of 15,000 within the ring equates to a potential market of 300 students. Keep in mind that a good school in a smaller market can pull much more than two percent. Still, that is a sobering thought.

What Demographics are Best for Your School?

A lot has been written about which demographics are best for a martial arts school. In virtually every case, the answer has been presented as though all schools are the same, so the answer has been a "one size fits all" answer. If you know anything about me, it's that I don't believe in "one size fits all."

The truth is that the best demographics for your school depend on what kind of school you are planning. You have to think through who your students are going to be, then study every resource in your area to find out their income, where they live, and how often they move.

Single-Family Homes

These have always been touted as the best location for a school, and that may be correct, depending on the school. For kids-oriented, family-type martial arts schools, being nestled within a community of single-family homes with a few elementary schools may be ideal. Elementary schools are packed (overpacked usually) with your target market, and they attract additional families to the area.

Multi-Family Homes

Multi-family homes are condos, townhouses, and apartments. Who typically lives there? Young adults, that's who. If your school offers adult-oriented mixed martial arts, self defense, kickboxing, fitness martial arts, sport, or just wants to pull more adults than kids, then you want to be in this kind of area. Bonus! What do multi-family home renters tend to do more than single-family home owners? Move! This means there is always a stream of new potential students unloading their moving vans everyday.

Large High-Income Homes

Because high-income families have large homes, there are far less of them in a given pull radius than single family or multi-family homes. Plus, wealthy kids have the resources to do almost any activity and often do. Your school may or may not be at the top of their list, even if they do join. Middle- and upper-middle-class students tend to focus on one activity.

That's not to say you can't make it work in this demographic. You can, like Keith Hirabayashi has with his school in Brentwood, California. You just have to be a really good, charismatic teacher, like Keith.

Your Potential With Your Pull

The Space

What is a good size for your school? It depends on the area and the rent. Remember, you want to build a profitable school, not your ego. Other considerations for the size of your school are: What segment of the market are you going for? Will you be able to schedule and support two classes per night, or five? If you only have two, you may need more room to fit all the students into just two classes. If you can support five classes a night, you will have smaller classes, which allows you to make a smaller space profitable much faster.

Kids take up less space than adults. It's better to lease a smaller space that offers the opportunity to expand than take a double space and regret it later. Always look for a space that has an empty space next to it, which gives you two benefits:

1. It makes your space more negotiable. Empty spaces mean lost money to a landlord. Also, it's harder to rent a strip of stores if some are empty. Traffic is the key, and empty spaces don't create traffic. Landlords are highly receptive to negotiation just to start filling some spaces. Keep in mind that the spaces may be empty for a reason. Make sure the space is in the right area and talk to all of the other stores in the plaza to see how the landlord is to work with and "how business is" at this site. Also, if you can, track down who was in the

space before. Ask them why they left and if they would rent there again.

2. It may provide you with a good expansion space when you are ready. The key is to include a clause that requires the landlord to give you first right of refusal at the same rent rate or lower as your current space. This way, if someone wants to rent the space, the landlord has to give you the chance to rent it first. Sometimes, the landlord will receive an offer that is significantly higher than your rent, and he will be motivated to rent it to the new client rather than you despite the agreement. In that case, you may be able to negotiate that you will allow him to rent the space, but only if he lowers your rent. If the numbers are right, he may be able to rent the space, lower your rent, and still come out ahead. Just make sure you won't need to expand before your current lease expires.

At the top of the size for new schools, my experience indicates about 4,000 square feet gives a new school plenty of room for a large training area, an office, and some changing rooms. On the other end of the spectrum, there are schools that do very well that have never expanded beyond 1,500 square feet. Any smaller than 1,500 square feet, and you may have to support a schedule with so many classes each day you will burn out quickly. Any larger than 4,000 square feet, your rent may strangle your cash flow.

Equipment

The martial arts school, provided it's not a Fantasy School, has a great advantage over health clubs in that we have very few and relatively inexpensive needs for equipment. What equipment you need depends on your type of school. If you are a family-oriented kids' school, a heavy bag will use up valuable space that could be used for students in class. On the other hand, if you are a kickboxing school, heavy bags are an important element of the school. In fact, one bag is usually not enough. There are companies you can hire to build multi-bag systems on frames that can be raised to the ceiling when not in use.

Here are some basic equipment needs for various schools. Go to www.martialartsteachers.com for our most current recommendations for suppliers.

Kids/Family   Body shields
                         Hand-held kicking/punching pads

Obstacle course elements (triangles, pads, tunnels, etc.)

Blocker pads (handle with padded shaft for striking)

Cones and obstacle pads for obstacle courses and races

Tape on the floor to show students how and where to line up

Kickboxing

Body shields

Hand-held kicking/punching pads

Heavy bags

Upper-cut bags

Jump ropes

Double-end bag

Speed bag

Body pads for partner to wear for striking

Self defense

Body shields

Hand-held kicking/punching pads

Fake guns and knives

Human-shaped freestanding bags

Padded mats for take-downs and throws

Kathy Marlor started with me as a 17-year-old former gymnast. She was a great student and an avid competitor who won a world title and became my highest-ranking black belt. More importantly, she grew into an excellent instructor and served as my right hand throughout the time I was running USA Karate.

I brought her on as Senior Consultant shortly after I created NAPMA. She now runs MartialCoach.com and works with Member Solutions. Despite her high profile instructor, she has certainly found her own voice and I couldn't be more proud.

Chapter Seven
Your Most Important Negotiation

No single element has to be more right than your rent. Getting locked into an expensive lease straps a school's cash flow every 30 days.

Rent is presented either monthly or annually. In Florida, a 3,000-square-foot space at $10 per square foot annually may rent for $2,500 per month; 3,000 x $10 = $30,000 ÷ 12 months = $2,500. A similar space in California may be presented at .83 per month per square foot.; .83 x 3,000 square foot = $2,499.99. As my dad always said, "It's the same thing, only different."

Rent is very much like a hotel room or a 30-second TV spot. Every day that goes by and the space is not rented is money that can't be recovered. That makes rent very negotiable. Make sure you are ready when you negotiate your rent. This section is designed to do just that.

One school owner reported that the realtor who found a space for him asked if he was a real estate investor, because of how well he negotiated the lease. The only thing he did to prepare was read my chapter on rent negotiations from *How to Open and Operate a Successful Martial Arts School.* Here is an updated version of those same negotiation techniques.

First, an important note: You will never be paid more in your life than when you negotiate. For instance, you are buying a widget. Instead of paying the sticker price of $100, you say, "Will you take $80?" He says, "I'll take $90." In the few seconds it took to do this, you made $10. Let's say it was a 15-second exchange; $10 for 15 seconds is the equivalent of $2,400 an hour. So let me repeat, you will never be paid as much as when you negotiate a price down.

How do you negotiate rent? After the initial walk-through, get an offer sheet from the landlord with his offer to you. Keep the entire negotiation process in writing. If, in phone conversation, you agree to a new point, confirm it in writing immediately to the landlord. It doesn't exist if it's not in writing. Don't assume anything; get it in writing.

Just Ask

The most important two words in business are *just ask*. You will never earn more money in a shorter period of time than when you *just ask*. In the leasing business, everything is negotiable, but only if you *just ask*. The answer is always no until you *just ask*.

The Flinch

Learn to physically react to any price. It takes some acting and some practice, but it's actually kind of fun and boy, does it pay well. Ask someone what the widget costs. Whatever they say, your response is, "What? You're kidding me! That's twice as much as I expected." Often, that's all it takes. The guy will drop his price or throw in something extra. At the worst, he knows you are "sensitive" to price. Warning: Tell your spouse what is going to happen. Once I flinched at a price, and my girlfriend at the time said, "I got so nervous when you did that. I could never do that." I had to explain it was all an act. Practice your flinch.

Walk-Away Power

This is the most important aspect of negotiation. You must convey to the salesperson that you are perfectly willing not to purchase, and you will walk out unless you get a good deal. Without this, any decent negotiator will hold his position, because it's clear you are going to buy anyway. In the car business, if the frustrated buyer storms out of the sales office to get in his car and go home, the salesman will chase him down. I even had one salesman step between my car and me to keep me from opening the door. I had to either laugh or choke him out. Either way, the deal always gets better at that point. If they let you go, the deal was as good as it was going to get that day. Either way, never get emotionally attached to a potential purchase. Even if you do, don't show it.

Higher Authority

This charade has been done to death in the car business. You make an offer to the salesman, and he says, "OK. I'll take it to my manager." The manager is the higher authority. It's the good cop, bad cop scenario. The salesman role is the good cop. He wants to find out what you like and see how emotionally attached you or your spouse are to the car. He will take that information back to the manager, the bad cop. You can be sure the salesman is not saying, "They are a nice couple, and this is a fair price offer." What he and the manager are doing is figuring how to get the highest price possible. The salesman comes back with a smile and a counter offer.

When you are negotiating a lease, be the good cop. Tell the seller you have to run everything by your people or your association. This gives you time to figure out your next move and keeps any emotional attachment out of the game. It also works to remind the salesperson that you are not the final decision maker and that the deal could get shot down at any moment by the association or your business partners.

Be Negative

It's never a good idea to walk into a space and say out loud, "This is perfect! We can put the changing rooms here, the pro shop here. This is ideal for my office...." By doing so, you expose your emotional attachment to the property. I am a very positive person, so let me say this: I am positive you want to be negative, or at least neutral, when negotiating a lease or even viewing a space.

Simply walk around, take some notes, do a rough floor plan of the shape, and tell the salesperson, "Gee, I don't know. This could be a lot of work." A good salesperson will start asking you questions then. Be sure to convey a very neutral position. "I guess I could make it work, but it's not going to be easy."

I said don't show emotion while looking at a space. Actually, you can do a little play-acting and show some negative emotion. It's an extended flinch. Communicate to the salesperson that if she wants you to go ahead with this, it's going to take some work on her part, starting with price and terms. Don't make it easy for her and hard for yourself; you're the one who has to make the monthly rent payments.

The martial arts industry is haunted with the ghosts of good schools that had everything going for them but ended up posting a "For Lease" sign in their window and closing their doors. One of the most common failures is a poorly negotiated lease that straps the owner with an exorbitant rent. A bad lease deal is not just high rent, either. Your start-up costs and your ability to expand can be drastically affected when you have a bad lease.

Signing a lease is like going into business partnership with a location and landlord for a period of time. Partnerships are seldom easy. Our goal is to help you turn this partner into a friend and not a foe of your future.

All leases have a basic framework that outlines how long you will occupy the space and how much it will cost you to stay there. Beyond that, there is a wide spectrum of lease structure. Don't think just because a term or condition is in the landlord's lease that it is carved in stone. Virtually every aspect of that lease is negotiable, and we've talked to many school owners who have received concessions they never thought possible by using our strategies. But they would never have received them – and you won't either – unless you just ask.

Be Prepared

Unless you know the current leasing conditions in your area, it's a good idea to get some expert help. Invest $100 for a commercial real estate attorney and/or commercial real estate broker known as a tenant rep. Their job is to help you get the best deal possible.

Landlords typically have their own attorneys, so it's smart to put your own team together. Tenant brokers can help you find a good location as well as offer ideas, insights, and experience on the current market, rental rates, and other conditions that may work in your favor.

Once a potential location is found, the rep can help you and the landlord come to terms on the key points of the lease.

Match the School with the Location

For a hard-core kickboxing gym, it would not make sense to rent a space in the middle of a neighborhood of kids and elementary schools. Conversely, for a family-oriented martial arts program with an emphasis on children, you wouldn't want to be in the downtown district.

Match your school with the demographics of the area. Before signing a lease, learn as much as possible about tenant history and why the other operations failed or moved. Speak with the current tenants about their experience with the landlord and the area. What is the make-up of the typical customer? Find out if any new building or road construction is planned that might affect your school's growth.

When researching a location, get demographic information on the area from your broker or the Chamber of Commerce. Know your Pull Radius and your Potential Ratio. Schools typically draw from a 15-minute driving radius, so start with that but don't limit yourself. You need to know the demographics for your immediate area as well. The farther away the demographic group, the less potential they have as students. Make sure you are surrounded with the right potential student base.

Finally, be sure the zoning in the area allows for a martial arts school. Know what limits you have on signage, parking, fire codes, etc.

Who's Going to Build the School?

Since the landlord owns the building, he commonly pays for any new structural elements of the building, meaning anything to do with the exterior. Tenants usually pay for all the lease-hold improvements, which includes interior areas, such as flooring, walls, ceiling, plumbing, and electrical within the space itself.

Keep in mind, the above is typical but, depending on the conditions of the market and the specific situation of the landlord, many school owners are able to negotiate an allowance or credit for improvements they make to the property.

School owners have reported from five percent to 25 percent per square foot in building allowances. For instance, if your 3,000-square-foot space is $10 per square foot (annually), and you negotiate for a 10-percent build-out allowance, you would have $3,000 in credits to build your school.

Typically, that would come in the form of free rent. So, in the above example, you would get the first month free ($2,500) and pay 80 percent of the second month, because you still had $500 of the credit.

These are actually very conservative numbers. In my second book, *How to Open and Operate a Successful Martial Arts School*, I tell the story of how I negotiated a $25,000 build-out for my second location, plus six months' free rent!

When you are negotiating a build-out, be sure the lease specifies how the credit is going to be paid. Will the landlord pay the builders, so you have no out-of-pocket expense? Will you pay, and then get a credit in free rent? That might mean less cash for start-up expenses but, as with everything in negotiations, it depends on your situation and on that of the landlord.

Also, make sure the free-rent period starts as late as possible and lasts for a specific number of days after obtaining your construction permits. If your build-out gets held up for a month because of permit delays, you will essentially lose the value of that month.

The great thing about a martial arts school is it requires little in the way of build-out. Unlike a restaurant or pub, you don't have strict regulations for equipment and food storage. Schools usually require little more than a padded open space, an office, changing rooms, and mirrors.

When entering into a negotiation, it's important to have a sound understanding of how the law of supply-and-demand applies to your situation. This will be the most influential condition of most negotiations for a lease. If you are looking at a strip mall with a lot of vacancies, it's clear the demand is not there, so these spaces will be less expensive and negotiations far more flexible than a busy, vibrant strip mall with only one vacancy.

Base Rent

The opening number offered by the landlord is usually the base rent amount. Because base rent doesn't include triple net expenses, it's a lower number, but it's not the real number you will pay each month.

Triple Net and CAM

Usually, base rent does not include insurance, taxes, and common area maintenance (CAM). These additional charges are called triple net. The base rent plus triple net equals your gross rent. Your gross rent is the check you will write each month.

Most leases, especially in larger plazas, are triple net. This means the tenants share in the expense of insurance, property taxes, and CAM. Many people confuse CAM with triple net. CAM is one third of the triple in triple net. It does not include the other two thirds, which are insurance and taxes.

When you are projecting your gross-to-rent ratio, you must include the triple net into the equation. You don't want to believe you are going to pay $3,000 per month rent, only to discover the bill is actually $3,500, because of $500 per month in insurance, taxes, and CAM.

Length and the Option to Renew

Length of your lease can get a little tricky. On one hand, you may want a long lease, so you can lock in a low rent and spread your start-up costs over a longer period of time. On the other hand, the longer the rent, the longer you are obligated to pay your landlord.

Often the solution is to negotiate a shorter lease, but include an option of first refusal on the space when the lease expires. This means that if the lease runs its full course, you have the first right to either renew the space or abandon it. If it's a really good space, you will want multiple options to renew. For instance, you may sign an initial lease of three years with three more options to renew at three years each. This way, if the school is doing well at this location, you know you will be there for at least the next 12 years.

This works best if you combine the Option to Renew with a three percent cap on any rent increase. Your lease might specify that you have the right of first refusal, and that if you opt to renew, your rent will not increase any more than the Consumer Price Index (CPI) for the previous year. The CPI works well, because it's universally accepted for determining rent increases and is published by the U.S. government annually, so it's easy to access.

This way, a landlord can't pressure you to leave by saying, "You have the option of staying, but your rent will double." The rent will not increase any more than the inflation index, which has been in the low double digits since the early 1980s.

Personal Guarantee

This is not always easy, but try to avoid putting a personal guarantee on the lease. If the school doesn't work, you would be personally responsible for paying the school's rent.

In most cases, you would be on the hook until a new tenant took the space but, in a bad market, that could be years. Furthermore, if the new tenant has a lower rent than you paid, the landlord could come after you for the difference. Worse yet, if the new tenant fails, the landlord may be able to go back to you to start paying again!

Try to limit any personal guarantee to the period of time that would cover the landlord for any out-of-pocket build-out expenses he or she incurred. This way, if the landlord pays $10,000 for your build-out, you will personally guarantee that amount, nothing more.

If you can't limit it to that amount, try to limit it to one year. Then say you will pay the rent in full for 30 days after you leave the space, to give the landlord time to find a new tenant.

Exclusivity

You do not want a kung fu school opening next to your karate school. Protect your market from competition with a clause that states the landlord will not rent to another martial arts school or a health club that offers martial arts classes. Try to get the restriction to apply to all of the landlord's properties within a five-mile radius. If the landlord balks, you can concede to the restriction just for the plaza you are in. But always get something in return for any concession.

Your Sign and Its Role in Marketing

Not only do you want to know what zoning limits you have on signage, you have to know what rules the landlord may have for signs in his plaza. Being in a great location is not good if you can't let people know about it.

Your school sign does more than alert traffic that your school exists. Your sign may attract potential students and give them an indication of what to expect. Here again is an element of The Core Dynamic, Value What You Do.

Deciding on what kind of sign and its design is a process as important as deciding on the interior design of your school. This is especially true for a new school seeking to make that critical first impression. Many established schools we see have old, worn signs that give the impression of a tired, worn-out school. The sign has lost its vibrancy and excitement. An old pub may be able to get away with a tired old sign, but a martial arts school thrives on excitement and energy.

Some new schools make do with a large vinyl banner, which clearly indicates the school is not only unestablished but also not too sure it will even make it.

A sign is an advertisement, but it's more than that. A sign creates expectations in a student or family. What expectations might a student create with an old, faded, or broken sign, compared to the expectations of someone seeing your clean, professional, well-kept sign?

A Worn Sign Signals

Low tuition (as in "low rent")
Lack of pride in the school
Owner does not care about image
School is outdated
School may be dangerous
School is unprofessional

A Professional Sign Signals

Higher tuition (professional fees for professional service)
Pride in the school
Owner cares about image
School is up to date
School is probably safer
School is professional

How to Choose a Good Sign

Step one is finding out what your local ordinances are regarding signs, then what your landlord allows. You do not want to make an investment in a big sign, only to have to take it down or pay a fine. Size, number of signs, lighting, colors, mounting, and the location are all subject to ordinance and landlord restrictions. The local sign-makers are usually on top of those issues; check with them.

How Long Should Your Sign Last?

As long as possible? Probably not. How long is your lease? If you move, can you move the sign with you? What if you are strapped for cash at the start-up stage and can't afford the sign you want? You may just need a good sign to get by until you can upgrade.

Universal Truths About Signs

Less is Best

Resist the urge to put too much information on your sign. What about a phone number and/or website? They can work, just make sure they fit into the design of the sign. Some schools are actually using the website url as the sign. For instance, NewYorkCityKarate.com would be easy to remember. You don't need the www. and you can make the .com small and a different color.

Bigger is Not Always Better

Not only are large signs harder to get approved, but they may also not be as attractive to the eye or, worse, could scream COMMERCIAL to the potential clients. Compare the golden arches of McDonalds to a local cafe. Who has the bigger sign, and what does it convey?

Good Signs Cost More for a Reason

Unlike much of your advertising, a good sign is a one-time investment. Don't go cheap. To get the best return on your investment on your sign, take the time, money, and effort to make it a memorable one.

Sign Visibility Chart

Letter Height:	Looks Best At:	Readable Distance:
4"	40 Feet	150 Feet
8"	80 Feet	350 Feet
12"	120 Feet	525 Feet
24"	240 Feet	1,000 Feet

Parking

Parking is a key issue that can work for you. You want to convey to the landlord that you will be bringing hundreds of people into his plaza or, in commercial real estate terms, an anchor tenant. An anchor tenant keeps the strip mall healthy by bringing in families who then shop at the other stores while they are there. An anchor tenant is valuable. That will make you very attractive as a tenant, as the landlord knows that the additional traffic you create will help the other businesses stay healthy and up to date with their rent. But if you don't have sufficient parking for those hundreds of people, you will be in big trouble.

In most cases, since we are mostly an evening business, the parking lot tends to open up for us as the other businesses close for the day. But don't take this for granted. Make sure you will have enough parking from 3 p.m. to 9 p.m. for all your students and families. On weekends, you may have events that require even more parking than during classes.

If you have 25 students in each class starting at 3 p.m., you will need at least 25 parking spots. However, when the 25 students for the next class arrive 15 minutes before the end of the current class, you now need 50 spots, even though it's just for a transition. Spending 10 minutes looking for a parking spot is not a good way to start class.

Lease Assignment

If you end up selling your school, be sure you are not restricted from assigning that lease to the new owners at the same terms.

Also, you may want to sub-let the space for certain classes during off hours. For instance, you may want to sub-let the space to a yoga instructor from 9 a.m. to 2 p.m., Monday to Friday, to offset your expenses and keep money flowing during down hours. Make sure your lease allows you to assign and sub-let the lease if needed. This usually requires landlord approval, but make sure your lease allows the possibility and specifies it will not be at a higher rate.

Should I Buy or Lease?

The basic rule of thumb is that, if you can buy for the same monthly price as your rent, it makes sense to buy. Even if the mortgage payment is a little higher (less than 25 percent higher), the additional expense is offset by the tax advantages and wealth building that owning the building gives you. Even if you are leasing, it's often a good idea to include an option to purchase the property.

Personally, I am debt adverse so entering into a mortgage for my business would be very uncomfortable for me. I would probably try to save as much as I could so I could purchase a building in full and then run the business rent free.

In the process of planning and starting up your school, few decisions will have as much impact on your prospects for success as choosing a good location and negotiating a favorable lease. Be careful not to get emotionally tied to any one location. Keep running the numbers to keep you focused on the potential upside and downside throughout the process. Stay cool, and most of all, don't forget to just ask.

Getting ready to blast some ribs in my first fight at the 1985
WAKO World Championships in London. Each fight featured three rounds of full contact with throws allowed. I
advanced to the gold-medal round after four fights.

We had a great team including Steve "Nasty Anderson,"
Linda Denley, John Chung, John Longstreet, Ray McCallum,
Tommy Williams, and Troy and Brian Dorsey.

Still, I never had a goal of being a great champion. I always
viewed competition as a way to make me a better teacher by
expanding my experience and perspective.

**The Truth About the
Martial Arts Business**

Chapter Eight
Trial vs. Non-Trial Enrollment Strategies

The trial program, in its many configurations, has been a staple in the martial arts school enrollment process for a very long time. A trial program invites the prospect to come into the school to try anything from a single class to a month of classes for free or a small fee.

A good trial program takes the pressure off of sales and onto teaching, which is where you want it. It's hard to get someone to enroll in your school for a year with just a visit. To do so requires more sales skills than most of us are capable of on a consistent basis. The trial program allows your teaching skills to do the selling for you. This is more comfortable for you and the prospective student.

We're going to look at a few proven trial and non-trial strategies and then discuss the process as it relates to your school.

Two-Lesson Trial Program

I have always advocated a two-lesson trial for $19.95 that includes a uniform. Essentially, I'm selling the uniform for $19.95 and providing the two 20-minute lessons as a bonus (you can get scripts to sell and teach the trial lessons at www.MartialArtsTeachers.com).

I like this process for good reasons. People who will pay $19.95 to take two lessons have already pre-qualified themselves for joining. Free lessons often bring shoppers, not buyers; in other words, people who are interested in martial arts but do not have the means to pay.

When people call, close on the appointment for taking the trial lessons and use a visit to the school as a fall back if they won't commit to taking the trial lesson course. This has worked at hundreds, if not thousands, of schools.

Guaranteed Enrollment Tour

In the early 1990s, Rick Bell of EasyPay introduced the Guaranteed Enrollment Tour as an alternative to trial lessons. This took the student through five stations that presented the benefits of martial arts to the prospect and finished at a custom poster that EasyPay had designed. The poster helped the salesman convey the benefits in a pretty emotional manner. If the student balked at the financial presentation, the sense of risk was alleviated by a 30-day money back guarantee. This was a far more sales oriented approach than the trial lesson process.

Information Kit

Andrew Wood used a hybrid approach at his Martial Arts America schools. Like the Enrollment Tour, this was more sales oriented. Andrew invited a prospect to the school to get an eight-page information kit. When the prospect arrived, the instructor invited him to take a trial lesson on the spot. This lesson concluded at the point the instructor felt the student was at his or her height of excitement. This was often a six- to eight-minute lesson followed by a presentation in the office for the close.

Member Referral

A successful strategy that involves free lessons has been done best by Bill Clark in Jacksonville, Florida. His concept is not a new one, but the execution is. He calls it the VIP enrollment process. He developed it with the help of Fred Mertens.

The concept is that the only way to join his school is to be recommended or referred by an existing member. That is not a new idea. However, he has taken this to a new level. He requires his staff to go into the community and strike up conversations with prospects in shops, standing in line, walking the sidewalk, in restaurants, and anywhere else they might be. The conversation determines if the prospect has any interest in training. If so, the staff member presents the prospect with a VIP card, which entitles her to a 30-day trial membership that includes a uniform at no charge. The instructor explains that the school only allows referrals in, so the instructor will refer her.

This has proven to be an excellent recruitment strategy. However, it does require a certain personality to approach strangers in the street about joining the school.

The strategy is to have them take two private lessons that are essentially the same as any two-lesson trial course. After the first or second lesson, depending on how well each went, an enrollment conference is made. The conference strategy is to offer three options for paying: a high monthly tuition, a slightly discounted tuition paid in five months, or a single payment with a significant discount.

This is a pretty standard presentation strategy, with the exception being that the instructor then offers to discount the membership further by crediting the value of the VIP pass off the annual program. So if the annual was $999, the student can reduce that $100 more by signing on that day. You would be amazed how many students will then cut you a big check.

Trial Month Offer

Tiger Shulmann Karate, arguably the most successful franchise in the industry, currently uses a $79 trial month offer that includes two private lessons and a uniform. Again, the idea is to enroll them after the two lessons.

After reading these strategies, you may be thinking, *that's what I do* or *that's a good idea*. Look a little closer. Reread them and you will notice that some of the largest, wealthiest, and most successful martial arts school owners in history use the trial lesson concept. Certainly, Tiger Shulmann and Bill Clark are in that picture, and your author has had a pretty good run in this business.

This is not to take anything away from Rick Bell and Andrew Wood but, for the most part, they dealt with small schools. Both are excellent salesmen, and that's an important requirement to make any non-trial introductory program work. You have to be able to close someone within 15 to 20 minutes of his walking in the door. Let me tell you, Rick and Andrew could sell. I know Tiger, Bill, and I could as well. I'm not sure our staff could, though, and I'm not sure all of you could. Selling is fun but not always easy.

The intro tour and the eight-page info book/quickie lesson put the burden of enrolling on the salesmanship of the instructor instead of the experience of the student. It's very difficult and a bit intimidating to have to make a decision to join a martial arts school within a half hour of walking in the door. It's like getting married without dating first. It's fast.

If you agree that the three dominant learning methods for the human population are divided into visual, kinesthetic, and auditory learners, you can be sure the kinesthetic will be hesitant to join without first physically experiencing the classes. That's one third of your market. The visual learner often needs time to go through your materials to help him get a grasp of what you are offering. That's another third of your market. The auditory learner may be best suited to listen to your pitch and act.

I'm not saying these are definitive percentages, and I don't believe anyone is 100 percent one way or the other. But the fact is that you would not buy a car without driving it first. I like people to know how we teach before joining. I want high-quality students, not only in terms of their ability to pay but also in their commitment to stay.

This is especially true if you are enrolling students into 12-month agreements when they join. Many areas allow people to cancel a contract before three days has elapsed. This is a "cooling off" period that allows people with buyer's remorse to get out of an agreement. Buyer's remorse is common, and we've all experienced it, whether someone persuaded us to make a bad purchase or we persuaded ourselves and wish we hadn't. The ratio of buyer's remorse cancellations for hard-sell enrollments is far higher than for more trial lesson based selling enrollments.

Imagine hard selling as the instructor on one side pulling a rope, with the prospect on the other side pulling back. He who pulls the longest usually wins. That's why car salesmen will babble on about anything and even step between you and your car to keep you on the car lot. They know the longer you are there, the more they will wear you down and the odds of closing you increase. It's not a fun process for either party. I know because I have pressure-sold many martial arts courses.

Much of this book is my updating, upgrading (shouldn't that be upGraden?), and sharing with you the awful truth about some aspects of this business. Here we go! Hide the kids. For squeamish readers, cover your eyes, and just peek because this gets pretty nasty. Most of all, don't try this at home . . .

Three of The Most Embarrassing Closes I Have Used

When all else fails, go to a third party to help the prospect make a decision – in this case, Benjamin Franklin, of all people:

"I can see you are having a hard time making a decision. Here's a technique Ben Franklin used to use. He would draw a line down the middle of a piece of paper and list all the positives to moving forward, and then he would list any negatives. Let's do the positives first. You will get in better shape,

like you said you wanted to. You will have more confidence. You said stress relief was really important to you, and you felt your health was not what it should be. When I asked you if you ever thought about being a black belt, you said it has been on your "wish list" for years. Of course, learning self defense ties right in with that. Let's see, that's one-two-three-four-five-six major positives if you enroll. Now tell me, what are the negatives?"

How about this for a hard close? I call it the "Back to the Future" close:

"Joe, I want you to close your eyes for a moment and just imagine what your future life will be like if you earn your black belt. You are in great shape. You're flexible. You're powerful, and you are getting high levels of respect and admiration from your friends and family. You have become a leader in their eyes. Now Joe, isn't that what you really want?"

Then there is the take-away close. I used this for years. You make the financial presentation and then add some artificial inflation:

"As a first-visit incentive, we will reduce the registration by $50 for enrolling today to make it easier for you to get started. So which program works best for you?"

I told you they were rough. Don't write those down. I know they are good, but only for parties. Don't use them...

If you have to use these 1980s closes, you didn't do your job in the trial lesson. This type of hard close often leads to buyer's remorse. No one likes to be sold, but everyone likes to buy. Trial programs take a lot of the buyer's remorse out of the process, because the prospect feels in control of the decision and has a clearer understanding of what that decision entails. It's more comfortable for him or her and a lot easier than drawing lines down the middle of papers or taking people on a contrived time machine. They surely know that any artificial $50 incentive will be available the next day as well as today. Wouldn't you?

Get on the Same Side as Your Prospect

After a good trial program, the paper work should be pretty easy. Imagine your prospect on his tiptoes at the precipice of enrolling, and you are behind him. With the most gentle, soft nudge in the back he or she takes the step. The closes above are more like a bulldozer trying to move a building. There is too much resistance, or you wouldn't have to resort to such non-sense. Promise me that if you use closes like those you will first put on a polyester suit with wide lapels.

Rather than a tug-of-war, collaborative selling is more like two of you on the same side of a huge rock, pushing it towards enrollment. If one stops pushing, the process is suspended until you both are at it again. This takes longer than a 15-minute sales pitch.

Martial arts instruction is a relationship business. Getting to know what your student really needs and how he can benefit from your school is an important building block of that relationship. At the same time, to be an effective instructor, you have to build the trust of your student so he will not just believe you but believe in you. The trial lesson is a big first step in accomplishing these important goals.

Twelve-month New Student Agreements collected by a good third-party billing company are best sold with a trial-lesson strategy. With good instruction and student service, a school following this plan should be able to build a solid receivable base that will make the cash flow more consistent and help the owner sleep at night.

My world-title match at the 1985 WAKO World
Championships. My coaches were Joe Lewis and Jeff Smith. After
two rounds, we were convinced I had it in the bag. I laid back in
the third round, which cost me the world title.

It was a crushing defeat but taught me a great lesson: the enemy
of success is complacency.

**The Truth About the
Martial Arts Business**

Chapter Nine
How to Teach a Trial Lesson

A Framework for the Introductory Course

This is a hybrid script. You will have to replace commands for ready position, ending, bowing, resting, etc., with your system's commands. Also, this is a mixed presentation. The language is more adult, but some references apply to children. Adapt this framework to your situation.

This is a 15- to 20-minute lesson, as is the second lesson. This can also serve as the core of a demonstration at a school. Instead of just providing entertainment at a demo, this is an excellent way to get your audience involved in the martial arts.

This class is best taught in a private or semi-private scenario, with the parents sitting there, watching. This lesson does not have to be taught by a black belt. Anyone can learn to teach this well with some practice.

Prior to the lesson, interview the student and/or parents to determine what they want out of the martial arts. You will see many areas where you can adjust this lesson to directly address those areas and clearly demonstrate how the martial arts at your school will benefit them.

This lesson can be presented as a $19.95 Introductory Course that includes a uniform. We prefer there be a charge for the course, as that works as a qualifier and is a major buying signal from the student.

I always want to give the student Instant Value in these lessons. I want them to have a series of exciting "Ahas!" This lesson uses the lead hand jab and front kick as the techniques. Students respond to these as they are obviously effective and pretty easy to do. We do not suggest you go into horse stances and forward walking stances in intro lessons, as they are not clearly effective or easy. The message with this approach is essentially, "Keep doing this and one day, you will appreciate how it works." That is Delayed Value. I want Instant Value to motivate the student to join.

The vocabulary for this lesson is probably for older kids, but you can adjust it up or down depending on who you are teaching. I taught mostly adults, so these are the words I used.

Notes to the instructor are in parentheses and sub headers.

Lesson One of the Introductory Course

Welcome to our school. My name is (your name). The style of martial arts you are going to learn is a very exciting system that originated in (your style origins).

It emphasizes a balance between mind and body. That balance is critical to every aspect of our training here. You will learn some very effective self defense techniques, which we'll balance with a strong sense of personal responsibility, so we never abuse or misuse our training.

The Importance of Black Belt is Taught From the First Class

Our goal is for every student to earn his or her black belt. That is an amazing accomplishment to be very proud of. These two classes will help us evaluate you, to make sure you fit into our program and will help you determine if earning a black belt is something you want to do.

To us, a black belt is not just about being able to fight and protect yourself. That's very important, but the best thing about becoming a black belt is how it helps you in every part of your daily life.

Black belt is a standard of excellence that everyone recognizes. You will often hear us say to do something "like a black belt." Since black belt is a standard of personal excellence and always doing your best, it would apply to more than just a kick or punch. For example, how would a black belt treat his parents? How would a black belt listen to a teacher? How would a black belt clean his room? That's what black belt is all about, and that's why we want our students focused on achieving their black belt.

The Two Most Important Techniques in Martial Arts

I'd like to start the class by teaching the two most important techniques in all martial arts, and probably in all areas of life. These two techniques are Respect and Focus. Repeat that with me: respect and focus. Remember that.

Not showing simple respect for each other causes much of the stress and problems in the world. In our school, we demonstrate respect in many ways.

For starters, we believe that it's not enough to have respect; it only works if you show it. All adults are addressed as Mr. or Ms.. If you don't know someone's last name, just ask. Everyone is very friendly here.

Also, all questions are answered with a "Yes, sir" or "Yes, ma'am" or "No, sir" or "No, ma'am." We'd like you to practice respect every day with your parents and your teachers.

So instead of saying "yeah," start saying, "Yes, ma'am" Got it? (they might nod or say yes or yeah). Oh! There we go. I think that was a good place to show respect by saying "Yes, sir" loud and proud. Let's try again. Got it? YES, SIR! That's better. You are officially on your way to black belt.

The next important way we show respect is the bow. A bow is very much like a handshake. Each class begins with a bow to show respect for the school, the instructor, and our martial arts system.

Here's how we do it. When the instructor says, "Joonbee," we snap to this ready position. Let's try it together. Put your feet one shoulder width apart, with your feet pointing straight ahead. Bring your hands across and snap them down to this position with your knuckles about two inches apart from each other.

When the instructor calls the Joonbee command, it's a command. It's not a request. You get your entire mind and body ready for what he is going to have you do by snapping to Joonbee with lots of intensity. Let's try it. I want to see Joonbee like a black belt! JOONBEE! Good.

Let's try one more time, JOONBEE! That's it. When the drill is finished, the instructor will have you return to this position very quickly. The instructor will either take you into a new drill or tell you to rest. If he says rest, turn around, straighten your uniform, and then return to the front and put your hands behind your back in an at-ease position.

The First Test

I told you earlier the two most important techniques in martial arts. What were they? (they may or may not remember. Usually they get respect, but not focus).

Hmm. This is interesting. You remembered respect, but you didn't remember focus. That's exactly why focus is so important. Good focus skills are critical to your success in the martial arts, in school, and in your career.

Focus is when you put all your attention and concentration on one thing at a time. I would not be a good teacher if I were not focused 100 percent on teaching you. It's also important that you are 100-percent focused on me, your parents, or anyone else who is teaching you.

It will be a while before you can kick and punch like a black belt, but you can begin to focus and show respect like one starting right now.

One way we show focus each class is when we are at Joonbee. We have our eyes focused straight ahead or on the teacher if he is speaking. No matter what happens, we don't move our eyes away. Focus like a black belt.

Locked and Loaded

Let's try it. JOONBEE! Rest. You guys can snap to Joonbee with more intensity than that. You don't get a black belt by accident. You have to work at it. JOONBEE! That's it. Eyes straight ahead (walk around students - wave your hand in front of their faces and snap your fingers). No matter what happens, you are locked and loaded. You are focused. Nice job. Rest.

Remember, on rest, out of respect you turn away from the instructor to straighten your uniform and then return to an at-ease position with your hands behind your back. Good.

This is when the teacher will be explaining what comes next. When the teacher is speaking, we show him that we are focused by keeping our eyes on him.

Plug the Master Instructor

Mr. Graden is a seventh-degree black belt, and what he teaches is very important. He's worked very hard to get the knowledge he is sharing with us, so it's important that we show him, or any other instructor, that we respect him and that he has our full attention.

We show the instructor that we are focused by keeping our eyes on him at all times when he is talking. Got it? Yes, sir!

Guard Rather Than Fight

In the martial arts, balance is everything. All of your techniques will be executed from a specific stance that is designed to keep you in good balance at all times. The first is Guarding Stance. Sometimes we call this Fighting Stance, but we like you to think of guarding yourself rather than fighting someone else.

You want to protect or guard the most vulnerable areas of your body. These are all right down the center of your body. They are your eyes, throat, solar plexus, and groin. One good shot to any of those areas can cause you a lot of damage, so we protect them. Guarding stance is designed to help you protect them and stay in good balance.

This is what it looks like. My feet are about one natural step forward and a little less than one shoulder width apart with my body turned to the side.

Turning to the side helps me protect my centerline. I bring my elbows in to the sides of my body and raise my fists up to my chin. Try to get your forearms parallel to each other rather than in a triangle, and turn the bottoms of your fists toward your opponent. Tuck your chin down to protect your throat a little more. As you can see, my weight is 50/50, so I can rock forward or back and can kick or punch with either hand.

Let's try it. Come to JOONBEE! Rest. Let's hit that Joonbee like we are black belts who are excited to learn. JOONBEE! Good.

Bend your knees. Bring your left foot half way in. Take a natural step forward with your left leg. We always step with the left leg first because our heart is on the left side. That's part of the spirit of the martial arts.

Turn sideways. Bend your knees a little so you're 50/50. Good. Bring your elbows in to your side to protect your ribs and raise your fists up by your chin. OK.

Sit forward a little on the front leg so you can begin to feel the stance. Back to center. Let's sit back a little. Good. Back to center. Now, let's drop straight down a little.

To get you to the other side, the instructor will command, "SWITCH!" When he says this, you quickly switch legs to the other side and get into your stance as fast as possible. Don't jump up; stay low and fast.

Second Test

Ready... SWITCH! SWITCH! SWITCH! DON'T SWITCH! (they will switch anyway). Ah. You must focus.

Remember, to end the drills, the instructor says return and then rest. Let's do that. Return!

(walk to the side – their eyes will follow you). Eyes straight ahead. Black belt focus. That's better; now rest. Any questions?

Our first strike is called the jab. This is one of the fastest strikes you have, so it's very important. First, let's talk about how to make a fist. In the martial arts, we strike with the first two knuckles. These are the strongest two knuckles, and the bones in your forearm support them. By using just two knuckles, we concentrate all the power of the punch into a smaller area. This makes it a more penetrating strike. It's very important that you keep your wrist flat, like this, so it doesn't buckle and sprain or break.

Reveal a Secret

The reason a small person in martial arts can hit with the power of a much bigger person is because all the power in the strike comes from your body weight, not just the weight of the arm or leg. Your arm may weigh five pounds, but your body weighs 30 times that (estimate based on student size). So we get our body power into the strike by turning our body when we punch. Watch.

In my guarding stance, with my hands up, the jab comes straight out from the chin. As it's moving, I keep my elbow down and behind the punch for power. At the last quarter of the punch, I push with my back leg and turn my body into the jab.

Notice I am tucking my chin down and raising my other hand up to protect against getting punched back. Then I snap the punch right back to my chin in a straight line. The shortest distance between two points is a straight line and the jab is a straight punch. Let's try it.

JOONBEE! Good. Let's move into our guarding stance. Left leg in, natural step forward, turn sideways, hands up. Let's start the jab.

The jab is always a front-hand strike. Keep your elbows down, and begin to extend the jab out. Now push a little off the back foot, and turn your shoulder into the jab. That's it.

Your hands have only two jobs. They are either attacking or protecting. Look at your right hand. Its job is to protect you right now, so make sure it stays up by your cheek with your elbow in to protect your ribs.

Tuck your chin down. Good. Let's try the other side, remembering to switch on command and get right into your stance. SWITCH!

Watch me as I snap the jab back and return to my guarding stance. Now you try it. Snap it back! Good. Let's jab again.

This time, let's do the whole jab, but I don't want you to push it out. I want you to snap it! Try not to muscle it like this. Instead, snap it like you were snapping a towel. Watch. Jab! Jab! See? Your turn. When I say Jab!, you fire and snap it back. Ready... Jab! Jab! Jab! SWITCH! Jab! Jab! Jab! Nice work. Return to ready! Rest.

Loud and Proud

To keep you focused during class the instructor might ask, "Eyes on who?" and you respond loud and proud, "Eyes on you!"

In the martial arts, breathing is a big part of how we create power, how we increase endurance, and how we stay calm in tense situations. When we fire a strike, we breathe out with a short, sharp breath from low in the stomach.

This gives you more power and snap and helps protect you by taking the air out of your lungs, so you won't get the air knocked out of you, since you have already pushed it out.

Let's try the jab again but with the added snap and power of good breathing. It looks like this (show three snapping jabs). Ready to try it? Yes sir! Good. Let's snap it like a black belt.

Joonbee! This time, when I say, "Guarding stance-step!" you'll step right into your stance just like this (demo). Ready... Guarding stance-step! Good. Body sideways and hands up. Jab with some snap and power. Ready... 1! 2! 3! 4! 5! SWITCH! 1! 2! 3! 4! 5! Good. Return. Rest.

The Fastest Technique of All

That was the jab. The jab is the fastest punch you can throw. When we move into drills, the jab is referred to as the number-one punch. You will learn a number of combination sequences that use numbers instead of punches, so remember the jab is number-one.

Front Kick

Your first kick is one of the most effective kicks in all martial arts.

The front kick is great for self defense, because it's pretty easy to keep your balance when you fire it. One critical element of every kick is how your foot is positioned. You want your foot locked in a powerful position, so it won't get hurt when you hit something. This is called the "blade" of your foot. Every kick has a blade.

Let's have a seat to learn how to blade your foot for front kick. Have a seat and extend your legs straight out from your shoulders. Turn your legs slightly in.

Point your toes and your foot as if you were going to punt a ball. This is a point blade. Now, without moving your foot, just pull your toes back.

See how the foot is straight and the toes pulled back? That is a front kick blade. When you strike with the front kick, you are hitting with the ball of the foot and pulling your toes back so they don't get smashed.

Pull your foot all the way back. Point. Toes back (repeat five times). Good. Now let's do the actual front kick.

Cue Words for Kicking

Every kick has four parts. They are:

1. Chamber
2. Kick
3. Recoil
4. Return to balance

For the front kick they look like this:

From my guarding stance, I bring my knee forward into a chambered position. Notice my foot is under my knee and not behind it. I want the foot to be moving toward the target at all times. Now, as I extend the kick, watch my hips thrust into the kick. That's the body power we talked about in the jab. This is the same thing. I want you to put your full weight and power behind the kick.

Notice I blade my foot on extension. To keep my leg from being grabbed, I snap it back and then return to my stance. So it's:

1. Chamber
2. Kick
3. Recoil
4. Return to balance

(Take them through front kick in the same sequence as the jab. Demo. Walk them through it. Have them solo slowly and then faster).

You guys have done a great job. You seem to really take to this. Do you have any questions?

Let's review:

1. What are the two most important techniques in martial arts? (Respect and Focus)

2. What system of martial arts are you learning? What is the name of your school?

3. What is the name of the punch we learned? (Jab)

4. What is the name of the kick we learned? (Front kick)

5. What stance did you learn? (Guarding stance)

6. What is my name?

7. What is our master instructor's name?

8. Eyes on who? (Eyes on you)

9. What is the goal of our students? (Earn a black belt)

10. If you want to do something really well, you do it like a (Black belt).

Great job, guys. Your next class is Thursday. Between now and then, I want you to practice your stance, your jab, and your front kick.

Practice only in an area where you won't hit anything or anybody, like your little sister. Do 10 jabs and 10 front kicks each day on each side.

On Thursday, you will learn another punch and another kick and take your white belt exam, which is pretty exciting. But we can't teach you something new if you have not practiced what we taught you this class. So you have to practice and practice like a black belt. That means with focus on correct form. That's the practice for your body.

Every Day in Every Way

We want to practice with our minds by showing focus and respect every day in every way. Keep your eyes on your teachers and parents when they are speaking to you, and always answer any adult with yes, sir or no, sir. Got it? YES, SIR!

Good. Class ends like it began. We come to Joonbee, bring our feet together, and bow. When we bow out, we say, "Thank you very much!" I thank you for working hard, and you thank me for teaching you.

Then we give each other a round of applause, and you are dismissed. Let's bow out. JOONBEE! Feet together. Bow! THANK YOU VERY MUCH! Applause....

Note: If this lesson has gone well, present the enrollment conference right after it. If the student enrolls, great, they move on to the second lesson. If they say they want to "think about it," you have a built in opportunity in the second lesson to resell them and offer them the opportunity to join again. Again, make sure you tailor these lessons to the benefits the parent or student has expressed interest in.

The Second Intro Lesson
We Don't Give Belts Away in This School

The goal of the second lesson is to enroll the student, so it has to be pretty powerful. In addition to teaching the back kick, reverse punch and reviewing the first lesson, we conclude the lesson with a white belt test. Remember, they are no-belts during this class. They wear the uniform, but no belt. We tell them, "At our school, we don't give belts away. They have to be earned and, at the end of this introductory course, you will take a test for your white belt."

The White Belt Exam

The white belt exam lasts about a minute. It's a three-technique test, and each has a number. Number one is the jab, number two is the reverse punch, and number three is the front kick. We stand in front of the student and call the numbers out. Their job is to fire the combinations we call. For instance, "One-two. One-one-two. Two-three. One-two-three."

We make it just hard enough to be a little challenging, and they usually make a couple of errors. We want them to make a couple of errors because, at the end of the exam, we salute, come to at-ease position, and say, "That was not a test of your physical technique; it was a test of the development of your black belt attitude. As a beginner, we didn't expect your punches and kicks to be like a black belt after just two classes. However, your attitude can change to a black belt attitude that fast. You're always going to make mistakes, but we're more interested in how well you recover from the mistake than the mistake itself.

In other words, the time I called, 'One-one-two,' and you went one-two-one, I noticed you repositioned yourself, refocused your mind, and prepared for the next combination. That is the black belt attitude. In other words, when you made that error, you didn't drop your hands, you didn't get frustrated, and you didn't lose your focus. You stayed future-focused, just like a black belt would. That's the attitude of success. So it is my pleasure now to present you with this white belt.

This white belt represents tremendous courage, because it takes a lot of courage to come out to USA Karate and get started. And if you work very hard and continue to come to class, in three to five years Mr. Graden will have the honor of tying a black belt around you. In between now and then the rest is up to you."

That's a very powerful finish to the introductory course. We've seen parents cry during that period; we've had spouses cry for a husband or wife who was taking a lesson. If it's done correctly, it is powerful. From there, of course, we move on to the enrollment conference where we will see how good a job we did of conveying the benefits of martial arts.

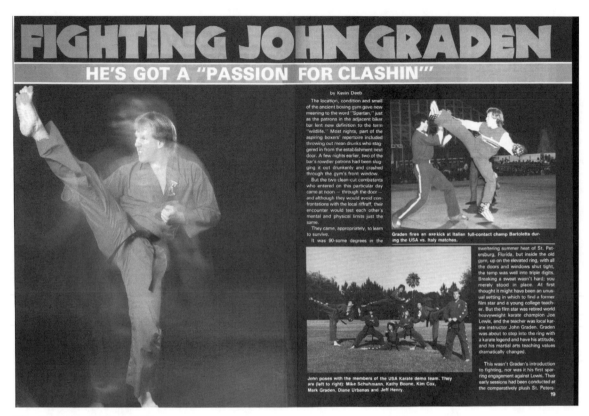

FIGHTING JOHN GRADEN
HE'S GOT A "PASSION FOR CLASHIN'"

by Kevin Deeb

The location, condition and smell of the ancient boxing gym gave new meaning to the word "Spartan," just as the patrons in the adjacent biker bar lent new definition to the term "wildlife." Most nights, part of the aspiring boxers' repertoire included throwing out mean drunks who staggered in from the establishment next door. A few nights earlier, two of the bar's rowdier patrons had been slugging it out drunkenly and crashed through the gym's front window.

But the two clean-cut combatants who entered on this particular day came at noon — through the door — and although they would avoid confrontations with the local riffraff, their encounter would test each other's mental and physical limits just the same.

They came, appropriately, to learn to survive.

It was 90-some degrees in the

Graden fires an axe kick at Italian full-contact champ Bartoletta during the USA vs. Italy matches.

sweltering summer heat of St. Petersburg, Florida, but inside the old gym, up on the elevated ring, with all the doors and windows shut tight, the temp was well into triple digits. Breaking a sweat wasn't hard; you merely stood in place. At first thought it might have been an unusual setting in which to find a former film star and a young college teacher. But the film star was retired world heavyweight karate champion Joe Lewis, and the teacher was local karate instructor John Graden. Graden was about to step into the ring with a karate legend and have his attitude, and his martial arts teaching values dramatically changed.

This wasn't Graden's introduction to fighting, nor was it his first sparring engagement against Lewis. Their early sessions had been conducted at the comparatively plush St. Peters-

19

John poses with the members of the USA Karate demo team. They are (left to right): Mike Schuhmann, Kathy Boone, Kim Cox, Mark Graden, Diane Urbanas and Jeff Henry.

The Power of a Good Photo

This is the splash page from my first cover story on *American Karate* magazine. Though you can't see it as well in black and white, the photo of the front kick is a blurred movement image with me in a red gi against a black background. This photo shoot was a huge success for me. I landed on at least a half-dozen covers just because editors wanted to use the shots.

I was in Berlin and showed a slide from this shoot to the publisher of an Italian magazine. He said, "If I can use this, I will put you on the cover." Not a single word was written about me in the magazine, but I got the cover.

I suggest you get a new set of PR shots every few years. Grow old with your audience.

Chapter Ten
A Baker's Dozen of Revenue Streams

To maximize your revenue, you must have a clear understanding of your revenue streams. Most schools operate with tuition, retail sales, and special events as their revenue streams. This is like driving a 12-cycle car with just three cylinders.

Read these carefully. Not all will apply to you, but wouldn't it be nice if they did? One clear requirement for successfully utilizing most of these is that you will have to use agreements rather than month-to-month programs.

Revenue Stream 1
Down Payments on New Student Agreements

Also known as a registration fee, this is the initial investment a student makes to join your school. Typically, this is at least two months' tuition. For instance, a program is $199 down payment/registration and $99 per month for 12 months or ongoing.

Revenue Stream 2
Down Payments on Renewing Agreements

This is the initial investment a student makes in order to renew or upgrade in your school. The best strategy for this has been the Black Belt Club. If you do not have a solid system for upgrades and renewals, this stream is dry for you.

Revenue Stream 3
Monthly Tuition

This is the lifeblood of your school. As you grow your school, your monthly tuition should grow as well. Ideally, your monthly tuition would cover your base operating expenses each month. For instance, if all the monthly expenses, including your salary, totaled $12,000, your monthly tuition collections from your billing company would cover that amount. In that very healthy scenario, these other streams are 100 percent profit. Mind you, this is not easy to accomplish, but even 75% of expenses paid from your billing check would be good.

Revenue Stream 4
Product Sales

Consider your retail shop as though it were a separate business. Open a separate business checking account for your retail, and deposit all gear sales revenue into that account. Use an American Express card or any other credit card that requires pay-off each month to pay for equipment purchases. When you place an order, pay for it with your credit card. This gives you up to 30 days to sell the equipment to your students. As they pay for the equipment, deposit the funds into the retail account.

When the credit card bill for the equipment is due, pay for it with a check from the retail account. Since you are usually doubling your money, this retail account will grow fast. Your credit rating will grow, as well as your rewards for using the card. Ideally, you will build a large cash reserve and save money on plane tickets and vacations, too.

Increase profitability by using MATA-approved vendors, so you can get the maximum discount. You can more than pay for your MATA membership with the savings our member discounts provide for equipment and other staples of school operation.

In addition, take advantage of the MATA Members' Online Proshop powered by Webmation. This program gives you the ability to sell thousands of martial arts products and supplies directly from your website. You choose which products to sell, set the retail price, and still only pay wholesale. Orders are automatically fulfilled and sent directly to your student's home. Veteran schools have reported that they have tripled their retail sales using this valuable service.

Best of all, student payments go straight into your bank account and you are billed your wholesale rate, allowing you to better manage your cash flow and not have to wait for your referral check to arrive.

I've worked with Hersh Sandhoo and his Webmation for years. This program is very popular

The Truth About the
Martial Arts Business

with our members. Go to the Members area of www.MartialArtsTeachers.com and click on Online Proshop to get more information.

Revenue Stream 5
Special Events

Even if you don't charge for testing, you will want to host at least one special event each month for your student body. These can range from nunchaku seminars to board-breaking, "Fear Into Power" seminars. These are not only pretty easy to manage, but they are a lot of fun. My nunchaku seminars were always packed with 30 to 50 students and would generate around $500-$1,000 per event. The fee of $25 included two rubber nunchaku to use in the class, so it was almost pure profit.

Let me tell you, I have an excellent Introduction to the Nunchaku one-hour seminar in me. I say one hour because, if I had to do 90 minutes, I would be in big trouble. Everything I know about the chucks can be taught in one hour. My point is that you don't have to be an expert to teach one of these special seminars. You have to know enough to keep the group interested, challenged, and having fun for one hour. Notice the title was Introduction to the Nunchaku, not Advanced Nunchaku.

Birthday parties would also go under this category. A two-hour $250 birthday party is not only a revenue generator, but also a lead generator. Some schools have at least one birthday party per week, so it's a proven winner. However, I personally have never done one nor would I. Kathy Marlor (MartialCoach.com) conducted all the birthday parties in our school and taught most of the kids' classes.

MATA has a section called Special Events that will give you strategies, promotions, pricing, and ideas for creating monthly Special Events.

Revenue Stream 6
Testing/Grading Fees

I didn't include these with Special Events, because exam fees are a little different from special events. Most exams for stripes occur in class, and they usually don't require a fee. The main graduations on the weekends require additional work and staff, so it's reasonable to charge for these events.

Typically, exam fees range from \$30 to \$50 and increase with rank. Black belt exams can be as much as \$200 to \$300 but, to justify this higher fee, it's a good idea to provide additional prep classes for the black belt candidates.

Some schools are large enough that they rent auditoriums to showcase their graduating black belts or to conduct the exam. The exam fee should cover these additional expenses.

Revenue Stream 7
Fast Track Testing

This is a touchy subject and has to be handled carefully. The idea is simply that some people are willing to invest more money to get through your belt system faster.

Most systems are set up for students to be ready to test every three months. Twice each week, the student takes a one-hour class, totaling roughly 24 hours of training between belts. Typically, about 15 minutes of class is spent on belt requirements, although sometimes it's more, sometimes less, and sometimes they are skipped altogether. Still, this works out to about six hours of work on belt requirements.

Fast Track Testing is a special program where a student pays a premium, such as \$199, to take a six-hour, one-day intensive workshop specifically on these requirements. At the end of the day, they take the belt exam. Before you throw the book across the room, let me make a point here: I have never done this, but that doesn't mean it's good or bad.

I think this can work well for certain belts but not so well for others. Accelerating a dedicated student through orange belt to green belt will not make much of a difference. However, I can't see accelerating someone through brown belt to black belt unless they were super talented.

One student, Glenn LaPlante, made black belt in 21 months with me, because he trained like a beast and was an outstanding black belt from the day he wrapped it around his waist. We didn't offer Fast Track Testing but, if we had, he would have used them and probably earned his black belt even sooner.

If you consider trying Fast Track Testing, please start with your lower ranks. Many ranks are really half-ranks anyway. For instance, orange belt broke up the time between white and green belt that traditional schools used. Orange belt is a retention rank. It has no universal standard. Gold or yellow belt is the same. These break up white to orange, so accelerating someone through certain ranks is an interesting and not altogether unreasonable proposition.

The Truth About the Martial Arts Business

You could make it available only for certain ranks, to ensure your students learn one of the key qualities of a good black belt: patience.

Revenue Stream 8
Paid in Fulls

Paid In Fulls (PIFs) have made a big comeback in recent years. Organizations like MASS have championed the cash out as a way of getting maximum revenue from a student base that is bound to drop out anyway. As much as I don't like the idea of treating every student like a potential dropout, smart use of PIFs can boost your bottom line significantly and MASS has it down to a science.

At its most basic level, a PIF is sold as a discounted membership. The student pays in advance for a period of time or a set amount of classes and receives a 20 to 30 percent discount for doing so. Some schools have made this their primary focus with new students. They offer significant discounts for paying in full. The VIP Pass program adds an additional $100 off the cash out price if the student uses it within the first few days.

As attractive as this may be – and let me tell you, some schools are racking up some amazing gross numbers doing this – there are some dangers that you must be aware of. Other schools have nearly gone out of business following the PIF strategies because they did not follow these important realities about PIFs.

Cashing students out works to the degree you:

1. Deliver what you sold.
2. Keep a steady flow of new students coming in. If everyone has paid and no new students are joining, your cash flow will dry up, creating massive stress. You must keep a stream of new potential cash outs coming in.
3. Are not a bloody fool with the money. Any bloody fool can spend money. When you first start doing lots of cash outs, you may be making more money than you ever have, and there is the temptation to buy a Mercedes or a new Presidential Rolex. But remember, if you have some slow months and everyone has cashed out, you will still have to pay the bills. Save the money and work toward buying a building for your school, rather than an expensive toy for your ego. Pay your rent in advance or stick the money in a mutual fund. Just don't get stupid and buy a new Mercedes to show off to your broke friends. Any

bloody fool can spend money. Don't be a bloody fool.

4.   Have an upgrade stream, so you can continue to offer new programs to current students who may have already cashed out on other programs. For instance, a student who cashed out a New Student 100 Class Program may do the same with Black Belt Club, Masters' Club, Leadership Program, or Career Development Program.

Revenue Stream 9
Renewals and Upgrades

Black Belt Club and Masters' Club are the most popular and proven renewal programs. They are covered in depth on MATA in our Renewals and Retention section, so be sure to research how they work there. For now, we want to focus on the renewal as a revenue generator.

Common practice has been to upgrade someone to a BBC or MC and replace his New Student agreement or program with the more expensive BBC or MC program. In most cases, the renewal had a registration of $299 or so, and tuition increased $10 per month.

Another popular strategy is to keep the student on her current tuition plan, but charge her a one-time or annual fee to upgrade to BBC or MC. For instance, a student is paying $110 per month for her current program. A BBC or Masters' Club upgrade is presented as an annual upgrade for $500.

Revenue Stream 10
Discounting a Past-Due Contract

When I was publishing *Martial Arts Professional* magazine, we sold advertising to clients who wanted to reach and sell to our readers. Occasionally, an advertiser wanted to cancel the contract. In the publishing world, the process for doing this is called "shorting the contract."

In exchange for committing to a set number of ads, the advertiser was given a discount for each ad. Shorting the contract meant that the ads the guy ran would be re-billed at the one-time rate and, if he paid the difference, we would release him from the contract.

For instance, if he committed to 10 ads at $2,000 each and cancelled after five, he would have paid us $10,000 of a $20,000 contract. However, had he purchased those ads one at time, the cost would have been $2,200 each. So, if he wants out of his contract, he would pay the difference between five ads at $2,000 (what he paid) and the single run price of $2,200. This would be $200 x 5 = $1,000. He would pay the $1,000 to "short out" his contract. It would be a fair deal for both of us.

You can use this idea in a similar fashion in your martial arts school. Say a student is halfway through a 12-month agreement at $100 per month and stops coming to class and paying. You can offer the student the opportunity to make the agreement good by letting him buy out the balance at a 40-percent discount.

In this example, he has $600 left, so a 40-percent discount would be $240 off, leaving a new one-time balance of $360. He would be allowed to return to class with all privileges and will also avoid having the billing company breathing down his neck (good motivation).

You may have to send a portion of that to the billing company (they will usually take it as a credit on your next check), but it's worth it. You got money that you most likely would not have, and your student is back in class and appreciative that you were willing to help him through a jam.

Revenue Stream 11
Discounting an Active Agreement

Read this only if you will not get greedy and sabotage your monthly cash flow for the lure of quick cash.

You can use this same strategy on a few students each month to boost your gross. Be careful that you don't offer it to more than just a half-dozen students. This is just one revenue stream. If you overuse this stream, it will dry up along with your monthly receivable stream. Keep the cash flowing! Remember, this is just to help your monthly tuition, not become your monthly tuition.

Call the student and tell him you have an opportunity for him to continue training at a significant discount. If he is interested, set an appointment to meet. Don't name the price right away, as he may reject you on the phone. Be prepared to do a little selling in person – just a little though.

Tell him to bring his payment method, as you only have a few of these to offer, and once you reach your number, it's gone. If you decide to do this, you need to do it right away, as we have only three of these. This is a true statement, because you want to offer this to only about six guys, of which three will probably go for it. If he asks why just three, you can honestly tell him, "Occasionally, I pick a few guys I know are doing good in classes and are here for the long haul. I think you are doing great, so I thought you would appreciate the opportunity to train at a discount. Of course, this is all confidential, but if you want to go over it real quick, we can do it before you come to class tomorrow/tonight."

If the student wants to do it but can't quite swing the payments, make it a 20-percent discount with as few payments as the student will agree to. If he has a $1,000 balance and can't cut a check for $600 today, but really seems hot for the idea, tell him you can offer him a short-term payment plan for $800. Ask him how much he can put towards the $800 today.

Whatever he pays, work out the shortest time frame for the balance. He may say $300. "OK, how long do you think it would take to finish it?" ("Finish it" sounds easier to do than to "pay off the balance"). Try to get him done in the next two months. You can explain this is designed for 90 days, which would be $250 per month for the next two months. Then he is finished with this program and can focus on his training.

This option may not be 40 percent, but $800 is still $200 less than $1,000. You can, of course, increase or decrease the discount level, depending on your situation.

To whom do you make this presentation? Depending on the situation, this may work best with a drop-out-risk C student. If a student is going to drop out, they may see this as a chance to "get out of the contract" at a discount. For you, it may present a chance to collect far more tuition than you would have had the student just dropped and stopped paying.

This is especially good for December when new enrollments are slow but typically jump in January. December is a good month to offer students the opportunity to cash out the balance of their program for a discount. I used 40 percent in this example but that may be more than you need to offer. As usual, the market will tell you what that figure is.

Revenue Stream 12
Career Training Programs

For years, I've taught the importance of creating a Leadership Team of assistant instructors to help you provide a higher level of service to your students. Typically, the Leadership Team is a "by invitation only" program for Black Belt Club members.

More and more schools are expanding Leadership Team programs into a precursor to a full-blown Career Development program that trains students to become martial arts school owners and instructors. Students pay for the right to attend staff meetings, practice role playing, and venture "into the kitchen" of the school.

Tuition for these programs are as high as $7,900 for a two-year course. Keep in mind that, in order to offer this, you really have to know this business cold and create a solid curriculum on par with a vocational school, because, in a sense, that's what you are offering.

Baker's Dozen
Student Audit

This is not so much a revenue stream as a way of plugging leaks in your cash flow. The Student Program Audit is a single sheet of paper with three columns and 11 rows. You can download a copy in the Downloads>Forms and Letters area of www.martialartsteachers.com. The columns are for a student's first, second, and third programs within a school. Typically, these are New Student, Black Belt Club, and Masters' Club, but any program will work.

The first six rows are the various payment options a student might use in your school. The next two are the start and end date for the program, which are followed by a check mark to make sure the Party Responsible for Paying is noted in the agreement and that the injury waiver has been signed. Your job is to audit each and every student's file to make sure you have each of these important items in the student's folder.

The first few times you do a Student Audit, it is like found money. You will be amazed at how much important paperwork is missing. More than that, you will be stunned at how many students are training who have expired or have no record of payments.

Staple one Student Audit to the outside of each student file.

My Admission of Omissions

Are there more revenue streams than this? Absolutely. Private lessons, speaking fees, community workshops, seminars for other schools, corporate fitness and/or self defense programs –the list goes on and on. This Bakers' Dozen, to me, are revenue streams that you can control day in and day out and within the four walls of your school. Certainly, private lessons are conducted in your school, but privates are usually more of a revenue trickle than a stream.

I have ignored one popular revenue stream and that is the afterschool program. While I applaud the entrepreneurial spirit of finding ways to create revenue, I have never run an afterschool program and I don't ever imagine I would. They make great money for the schools doing them and it seems they are providing a valuable service. But, going back to The Core Dynamic of Finding Your Own Voice, I just don't see that as part of what I would want to do in the martial arts.

A Short Rant

To me, afterschool programs are like the XYZ "Gymkata" we see in tournaments today. It seems desperate and removed from core martial arts. I'm happy to see Tournament Forms finals on ESPN, but I have never been able to watch an entire show. I get disgusted and turn it off. I personally do not see what sticking a flip in between a half-power side kick and a half-ass punch in a shallow balance have to do with kata. End of rant.

Build Around Your Core

Not all of these revenue streams will be for you. That's why the Core Dynamic of Finding Your Own Voice is so important. I personally helped create many popular trends in this industry. I also made it clear what programs I would never teach, even though I developed and sold them. What is good for me may not be good for you. Know what you like, and why you are doing this for a living, and then build strong revenue streams around those core programs.

The Truth About the
Martial Arts Business

Joe Lewis and I teaching a seminar in Florence, Italy.
Actually, he taught and I got hit a lot.

I was with the USA Team on a tour of Italy when we
arrived at this resort in Florence the night before. Our
hosts escorted us to a huge banquet hall, where we
entered through large double doors.

We were surprised to see it full with hundreds of martial
artists in uniform. They all stood and gave us an ovation
as we walked through to our table on the main stage.

The gentleman behind me in white gi pants is Ennio
Falsoni, long-time President of the WAKO.

**The Truth About the
Martial Arts Business**

Chapter Eleven
How to Set Your Tuition

In 1974, the tuition at the Florida Karate Academy in Largo, Florida, was a 12-month contract at $25 per month. If you just raised tuition three percent per year from that point, you would have tuition of about $60 per month in 2004. When I opened my school in 1986, my tuition averaged $75 per month. At three percent inflation, this would total $127 per month today. What other service has only increased three percent per year? Not many that I can think of.

While many schools are more in the $60 range, others are north of $200 per month. What is the difference? Remember the Core Dynamic of Value What You Do? The most successful martial arts school owners highly value what they do. Tiger Shulmann said this in an interview in my *Martial Arts Professional* magazine in 2001: "I'll give you an idea of what I think about the amount of money that we charge for our classes. $1,500 doesn't scare me at all to charge for martial arts training. I think it's too little, actually. But we have to stay somewhat within the industry's standard."

His implication is that he would charge more, but the industry is holding him back. Tiger clearly values what he does. All the top school owners do. Notice that the first thing he said was he was not scared at all to charge $1,500 for training. Was he also saying other people might be scared to charge that amount? Would you be scared? This is a guy who told me he had more than 20,000 students in over 35 schools at the time. I visited his headquarters and saw the August revenue gross numbers from all the schools on the computer. It was only the third week of what is typically the slowest month of the year, but the lowest gross was in the mid-$30,000s, and the highest was the mid-$90,000s.

Not only was Tiger not scared to charge higher than the competition, the market was not afraid to pay for it either.

Your tuition rate and how it is presented will play a fundamental part in your school's image. Price is the main factor in a prospect's decision to join *if you* make it the main factor. If the most compelling reason for someone to join your school is that you are cheaper than the next guy, you are putting all of your eggs in the wrong basket.

Price is a factor, but not the factor in whether the prospect moves forward to join your school. If a prospect has shopped other schools, then your tuition will naturally be compared to the other schools. That doesn't mean the lower price wins. It's just another point of comparison. If the prospect has not shopped other schools, and most do not, your tuition indicates the value you and your current student body place on the training. It also begins to establish in the prospect's mind what to expect in the school.

The Lower the Price, the Lower the Expectations

When you read this sub-head – the Lower the Price, the Lower the Expectations – what came to mind? Did you feel that meant that the market would have lower expectations of your school if it was low price? Or did you feel you would not have to meet high expectations if your price was low? For far too many owners, the second description is more accurate.

As your skills as a teacher improve and your system for operating the school becomes more polished and professional, you can begin to raise your standards of performance and your tuition with it.

This is not to say people don't like a good deal. Everyone does. However, there are certain things you don't expect to have discounted and, in fact, may not want them if they are. Health care is at the top of that list. Rarely do we say, "Give my kids the cheapest medical exam possible." Education is much like that. Parents don't work hard to give their children the cheapest education possible. Your martial arts school is not a gym where club owners compete over $29 membership fees. You want to be compared to the local private schools, not the local gym.

In establishing your tuition, divide your area's pull potential student base into three levels of income: the lowest third, the middle third, and the highest third of income earners. You want to price your tuition for the middle and highest thirds, not the lowest. It is much easier to manage quality and teach 100 students paying you $150 per month than 300 students paying you $50 per month. The gross is still a projected $15,000 per month, but the amount of work and stress to manage 300 students is much more than just three times what it is for 100.

The top two thirds of income earners are not terribly concerned over $100 or so one way or the other. They are concerned about getting a return on their investment and feeling as though they are valued members of your school. They will also want to train with people in the school who are like them and want to be trained by a staff of professionals.

The Screen Money Provides

To a degree, the high-income earners' market will want to train at a club that not everyone can afford. This is not out of snobbery as much as the natural screening process that money affords them. This is why people belong to country clubs and private golf courses. I've belonged to plenty of each, and usually they are not any nicer than upper-scale public facilities. The difference is that by paying more for what everyone else can have for less, you don't have to do it with everyone else. The levels of expectation are much higher for the private club, and so is the price.

The School Down the Street is Cheaper

Here's a great response to a prospect that points out that the school down the street is cheaper: "Mrs. Jones, we could charge that same tuition. But you know what? We would be packed, and it would be a lot harder to give your son personal attention and to maintain the quality of students we are known for. Plus, it probably wouldn't be as safe with loads of kids in here on a discounted program. We're all about quality, and our tuition helps us keep our student standards high. Our school is really for the families who want the best for their children."

Don't you love that last line? "Our school is really for the families who want the best for their children." What parent is going to respond, "Well, that's not us. We want less than the best for our kids."

The most important thing to understand is that this market will not expect you to be the best instructor and the cheapest at the same time. However, at a good price, they will expect you to be the best, so make sure you are always studying and expanding your skills as a martial artist, a teacher, and a businessperson. Then, make sure you are training your staff at least two hours per week to carry out the mission of Being the Best.

How Much Is Your Tuition Really?

This is a little drill that can make grown black belts cry. Here is an audit you can do to help you understand how much tuition you are really collecting each month per student.

1. Total Tuition Collected: Take last year's total tuition collections. This is the sum of paid-in-fulls (PIFs), registration fees (uniform or any other hard costs deducted), and monthly billing received (after deducting refunds and any billing and credit card charges).

2. Total Student Count: Add all the students you had last year on January 1st to the number of students you enrolled over the next 12 months. If you started the year with 100 students plus you enrolled 10 new students per month (10 x 12 months = 120), you have a grand total of 220 students. Of course, unless you have 100-percent retention, you don't have 220 students in your school right now, but that's a different chapter.

3. Divide last year's total tuition collected (1) by the total student count (2). This is the annual tuition value of your students

4. Take that number and divide it by 12. This is the average monthly value of your students. To be more accurate, you would do a month-by-month analysis that removes the dropouts as they stop paying. That would make the average monthly value higher, but this example is designed to be easier to understand and follow.

Let's use real numbers. I'll keep the money high and the expenses low to soften the blow.

1. Last year you averaged 80 students paying $133 per month in your school. You also have 30 students who cashed out last year or "shorted out" their contract (see the Baker's Dozen of Revenue Streams).

a. 80 x $133 = $10,640 per month gross.

b. Billing fees, refunds, etc. = 10% in expenses (Billing is in the 7-8% range, but if you add in refunds etc the number can get closer to 10% total)

c. Net monthly billing: $9,576

d. $9,576 x 12 = $114,912 total monthly billing

e. + Total "shorts:" 30 @ average $600 each = $18,000

f. Registration fees: 105 x $199 = $22,885

g. PIFs for annual: 15 @ $999 each = $14,985

h. = Tuition total: $170,782

2. Students taking class last year

a. 100 students to start with

b. Enrolled 10 per month = 120

c. 100 + 120 = 220 students who took classes last year

3. Last year's tuition per student per year

a. $170,782 ÷ 220 = $776.28 per student per year

4. Last year's tuition per student per month

a. $776.28 ÷ 12 = $64.69 per student per month

It's kind of scary when you realize how much of a hit your tuition takes. Keep in mind these are pretty simple numbers with a too simple formula. The real truth is that often the numbers are worse. Family discounts, cancellations, barters, and students who slipped through the cracks all bring the average tuition per student number down.

What can we do to pump these numbers up? You may have noticed that we didn't include any renewals. The reason is simple. Most schools still don't have a solid renewal plan. The best renewal plan I know of is also the most important to your school's energy and atmosphere, and that is the Black Belt Club or the Black Sash Club or whatever you want to call a program where the students set black belt as their goal (and you don't guarantee it).

1. Let's take the same example as above, but add in the revenue from renewals.

a. Tuition total from above = $170,782

b. + Renewal registrations: 24 x $299 = $7,176

c. + Renewal PIF: 5 @ $2,999 = $14,995

d. = Tuition total: $192,953

2. Students taking class last year

a. 100 students to start with

b. Enrolled 10 per month = 120

c. 100 + 120 = 220 students who took classes last year

3. Last year's tuition per student per year
a. $192,953 ÷ 220 = $877.05 per student per year

4. Last year's tuition per student per month
a. $73.08 per student per month

Total difference in net tuition collected = $22,171! Still, the number is far less than the average monthly tuition you are charging.

Still, if you have been procrastinating about launching a Black Belt Club, I have 22,171 good reasons for you to do it now. Many schools have gone from an agreement-based renewal program to offering the Black Belt Club membership for an annual one-time payment of $500. Regardless of how you charge for Black Belt Club, it will add a significant amount of revenue to your school.

My *USA Karate* television program aired for a decade in the Tampa Bay area, which is the 12th largest media market in the USA. It was by far our biggest source of students.

Joe Lewis was my first guest when the show launched in 1987. My anxiousness as a first time host showed when I turned to the camera and said, "My first guest is a former world champion and was named the greatest fighter in the history of karate. Please welcome Chuck Norris."

Everyone laughed but Joe and I.

The Truth About the
Martial Arts Business

Chapter Twelve
What It Costs to Get a New Student

Take a moment to write down all of the expense, effort, and energy that goes into attracting and enrolling new students. Here's a short list of the resources necessary to turn a stranger into a student:

1. Time to create marketing plans
2. Capital to purchase ads, print flyers, etc.
3. Time and stress to execute marketing plans
4. Time, stress, and money to train your front line staff to set and confirm appointments from the inquiries resulting from your marketing efforts
5. Time, stress, and money to train your staff to teach intros to those appointments
6. Time, stress, and money to train your staff to conduct enrollment conferences
7. Time, stress, and money to train your staff to collect the tuition for these new students
8. Payroll for the staff to carry out 4 through 7

Let's take a look at some real-world numbers.

Imagine a funnel representing your marketing efforts. You pour risk capital, time, and stress into the top of the funnel and, hopefully, black belts come out the other end. The better job you do marketing, the wider the top of the funnel. The better job you do handling the front-end process of turning phone calls into good appointments to take an intro and, later turning intros into enrollments, determines how wide the funnel continues to be.

These first four levels all the way until enrollment take a tremendous amount of effort. Of course, how well a job you do in terms of teaching, retention, and student service will determine how wide the bottom of the funnel is.

Despite all the money, time, and stress, you don't actually get paid until the fourth level, and that is only if a student enrolls. You don't get paid to market. You don't get paid to take phone calls. You don't get paid to set appointments or teach intros. You only get paid when a student goes through that process, signs on the dotted line, and hands you a credit card or check.

As a standard of performance, each level should result in 80 percent of the level above it. If you get 10 calls from an ad, you should set eight appointments (80 percent) and have six or seven intros resulting in at least four or five new students. A similar gauge is that you should be enrolling 50 percent of your phone calls.

Let's look at this process in real numbers. You will see how easily a school can lose money or just simply break even by the time they enroll a new student.

In this example, you've invested $1,000 for some type of marketing, but how you spent the $1,000 is not the focal point of this illustration. What happened after you spent it is.

The Conversion Ratio is the percentage of people you move from one level to the next. In the three columns are three sample ratios ranging from the good, the bad, and the ugly. Though each school invested the same amount of money in marketing and received the same number of phone calls, the results are strikingly different.

$1,000 in Marketing	Good (80%)	Bad (65%)	Ugly (50%)
Phone Calls ▷	40 = $25	40 = $25	40 = $25
Cost per Appointment ▷	32 = $31	26 = $38	20 = $50
Cost per Trial Lesson 1 ▷	26 = $38	17 = $59	10 = $100
Cost per Enrollment ▷	20 = $50	11 = $90	5 = $200

50-Percent Conversion Ratio (The Ugly)

Each example invests $1,000 in the same marketing areas. The investment risk is the same, but the return on that investment is very different.

The right column is a recipe for disaster, yet all too typical. Though this school has done a good job of keeping its cost per call down to just $25, the cost doubles to $50 per appointment because only 20 of the calls are actually set appointments.

Think how easily this can happen. How many calls come in that are not answered or not returned? How many calls does an untrained person answer? How many so-called "appointments" are really weak promises to stop by? If you track these numbers – and the best schools track them daily – you will see how easily you can land in this dangerous 50-percent rate.

Make sure you and anyone else who answers the phone or responds to an inquiry about lessons is fully trained and understands that the goal of the call is to set a solid appointment to come in and take an intro class.

In the 50-Percent Conversion Rate column, only half of the appointments set actually take an intro lesson. This means each intro costs you $100. We've checked around, and no one is charging $100 per intro. At the 50-percent conversion rate, you are going in the hole. Sadly, it gets worse. When only 50 percent of those intros actually enroll, each new student costs you $200. If you get $199 as a registration/down payment, you've gone through an enormous amount of stress to profit $1.

Again, most of you are not tracking these numbers, but if you did, I would bet a steak dinner you are in the 50-65 percent range for conversions. Sure, you may have a 90-percent intro-to-enrollment conversion rate, but if you are at a 50-percent call-to-appointment and then appointment-to-intro, you will still be within the overall range of 50-65 percent.

65-Percent Conversion Ratio (The Bad)

In the middle column, a significant bottom-line difference results from just a 15-percent improvement in your Conversion Rate. Though the conversion rate is still not as high as you want, the cost per new student is significantly less. This small 15-percent increase in performance yields a huge reduction in your cost per student.

You can see that small improvements yield high results, especially as they are compounded over time. In this example, a 65-percent conversion rate will enroll about 72 more students over a 12-month period. As you will see in the next example, an 80 percent conversion rate will result in nearly 200 more enrollments in a 12-month period over the 50 percent rate and about 120 over the 65-percent rate.

80-Percent Conversion Ratio (The Good)

Take it up another 15 percent, and you get to the 80-Percent Conversion Rate column, which is where you want to be. Every step of the way towards converting a stranger into a student is less expensive. Of course, it's not profitable until the student enrolls, but in the 80-percent range, your cost per student is one-quarter that of the 50-percent rate at just $50.

I'd write $50 checks until my hand cramped up if each check would put a new student on my floor. I'd be less enthusiastic at the $90 (65-percent) level, and I'd find another way of making a living at the 50-percent level, because I'd be starting off too far behind with each student. If I have to pay $100-$200 per new student, the students have to be into their second or third month of tuition before they become profitable. That is an exercise in frustration.

That's a stressful way to do business. As clear as this illustration is, many owners do not track these numbers. It's not that they are lazy; they really don't want to know how bad a job they are doing at converting strangers into students.

Typically, the owners say things like, "Once we get them in the door, just about everyone signs up." They complain marketing doesn't work in their area, or that the economy is bad, or that the belt factory school down the street is selling black belts or – my favorite – "We're not a commercial school." The truth is that they are paralyzed by the Control Factor and would rather protect their little puddle than take the time and risk to the ego to learn how to set appointments, teach smart intros, and close on an enrollment conference. In short, they are afraid to ask for the check. Re-read Value What You Do.

MATA has excellent resources and scripts for this entire process, so getting the good information is not the challenge. The challenge is breaking out of the box to use it.

Many owners say they just want to teach. They don't like the business of selling. They want someone else to handle the conversion process. That's understandable; however, you must learn how to sell first. Otherwise, who is going to train your front-line people?

You can't print out a few pages from MATA, hand these to your employees, and expect them to keep an 80-percent conversion rate. You have to know this process inside and out, so you can teach it like a professional martial artist.

As the school owner, you have more interest in creating a solid process for converting students into strangers than anyone. If you don't care enough about your business to learn, role-play, and train how to improve this system, no one else will.

**The Truth About the
Martial Arts Business**

Tony Robbins on John Graden's Successful TV Show "USA Karate"

Anthony Robbins was a guest for five interviews on my *USA Karate* program. He earned his black belt with Jhoon Rhee in eight months. For this photo, I suggested we both put our guards up. He said he wanted to project a more peaceful pose.

At the final NAPMA World Conference in 2003, we presented him with a Lifetime Achievement Award. He sent us a 45-minute motivational speech geared towards martial arts. He walked on camera, bowed deeply, and said, "Hello, NAPMA."

A few months later I had to say, "Goodbye NAPMA."

Chapter Thirteen
Agreement vs. Non-Agreement
Student Programs

A school is a membership-based business model. The majority of a martial arts school's revenue comes from students' tuition, which is normally paid monthly. A school that attracts and keeps students grows this monthly income. You will have other profit centers and revenue streams such as retail sales, special events, and testing, but tuition is the financial foundation of any school.

Your school's financial stability will at first be dependent on growing this monthly tuition revenue. This is called building your base, and it is important. Let's look at some of the issues and processes involved.

Contract vs. Month-to-Month Tuition

This is an age-old argument, and the answer has changed somewhat with technology. First a word about unpaid tuition. Under no circumstances do I suggest you ever sue a student over unpaid tuition. If you have a student on an agreement, and she quits after six months, don't begin a hard collections process. Rarely will you collect much money for the stress and effort. Nearly 100 percent of the time, however, you will have someone in the community telling other people what a louse you are.

That said, the argument for using an agreement for new students holds up better than for using a month-to-month program. Here's why. Students who sign an agreement (we never say contract, do we?) are entering your program more committed than students who know they can quit at any time. Even if they do drop out, they tend to stay on longer to try and make good on their agreement. This is especially true if you have done a good job of qualifying the prospect and helping him understand the importance of the commitment.

One of the Core Dynamics of the Martial Arts Professional is to Value What You Do. Using an agreement reflects this. It shows that you have a process for bringing students into the school. Like a private school, your agreement process allows only people on your floor who are mentally (and legally) committing to training with you for a year. You are a highly trained, specialized, teacher. Here is the value perspective from the instructor's standpoint:

It is a waste of your time and energy to pour your heart into a student who is only going to drop out after a few months when football season starts.

Through the years, the firmest advocates of contracts, or agreements as I prefer to call them, have been the billing companies.

EFC and Nick Cokinos

In the 1980s, Educational Funding Company (EFC) was the first to have success creating systems to support an agreement-based school. Our industry owes a debt of gratitude to Nick Cokinos and his ability to teach, motivate, and inspire some of the most successful school owners today. Guys like Dave Kovar, Steve Lavallee, and Keith Hafner all learned the business from being clients of Nick Cokinos.

Mr. Cokinos was an early partner with Jhoon Rhee, and together they created many of the business elements we take for granted today. From the Black Belt Club to musical forms and safety equipment, the ideas that came out of the powerful combination of Jhoon Rhee's drive to make a difference and Nick Cokinos' business savvy created probably the most successful family tree of martial arts school owners. Jeff Smith, Stephen Oliver, John and Pat Worley, and Regina and Angel Gonzalez may not all have been EFC clients, but they cut their teeth as students and then instructors under Jhoon Rhee while Nick was running the businesses.

EFC emphasized having systems for every aspect of your school and building your receivables base as the way to build wealth and value for your school. As self-serving as this may seem coming from a billing company, they are absolutely correct. That's not to say many cash out kings and month-to-month schools have not built personal wealth, but it's tough to build value in your business if the majority of students have already paid or are free to leave at anytime.

If your exit strategy is to sell your business, then this is something to consider very seriously.

Not many people are in the market for a school full of students who require lessons but have already paid. Month-to-month schools can be sold but will usually not get the same price as a school with a portfolio of agreements and a history of high collections.

Having an agreement is also good for retention. That's not to say students on agreements don't drop out; they certainly do. However, the very nature of making a contractual commitment to train for a period of time helps students stay longer than those who can cancel at any time. Some school owners dread presenting an agreement to be signed by a new student. Conversely, the instructor who understands the Core Dynamic of Valuing What You Do feels it is a waste of everyone's time for someone to enroll for less than 100 classes or about one year. What would someone get out of three or six months of martial arts? If you are a top instructor, you want to work with students who appreciate that and will be in class.

Remember, in almost all markets, the largest schools with the most students and highest tuition typically require agreements. Often these are surrounded by smaller mom-and-pop schools or dungeon dojos with signs in the window reading "No Contracts." The sign should say "No Confidence." Not that every school that doesn't use contracts lacks confidence. I mean that a school that uses that as its unique selling position is selling from a weak place.

Using an agreement tells prospects that you have expectations about your relationship. It communicates that you Value What You Do, and that is a positive element in helping the student gain confidence in your school. Certainly, an agreement can complicate the enrollment process, but not as much as many might think.

The Key Attitude in Enrollments

Like all sales – the most successful ones start with an attitude of resilient optimism. The successful salesperson believes in what he does, and he believes everyone will enroll. This is much bigger than you may think. People who are nervous about contracts will often convey that to the prospect, who will then "contract the virus" of concern.

Proficient salespeople are very well rehearsed, and they understand people. They don't make light of the agreement; they also don't concern themselves with it. It's just the final step in the enrollment process. They simply present it as an opportunity for the student to get involved in the school. On the other hand, the struggling salesperson will present it as though the student were signing her life away.

It makes sense, though, in a business like martial arts where there is still confusion and concern about money mixing with arts, that the promise of high enrollments without agreements would be very attractive, and it is.

EasyPay and EFTs

Larry Dokes's EasyPay billing company pioneered the electronic funds transfer (EFT) in the early 1990s. Larry was an early mentor of mine and has helped me a great deal. Based in Belton, Texas, EasyPay specializes in smaller schools in smaller markets. EasyPay offered a non-contract solution that automatically withdrew students' tuition from their bank accounts. This took most of the monthly decision of who to pay out of the students' mind since the tuition was automatically paid.

EasyPay made a good argument that schools who do hard collections for unused lessons are creating big problems for the entire industry that might even lead to government regulations. I agree. While some soft collection is fine for agreements, moving to the point of hard collections – especially where the student's credit is negatively affected – is not usually a good idea for your reputation or that of our industry. Teaching better classes is a more productive way to invest your time and energy than hammering students you were not able to keep.

The original appeal of the EFT was that, if a student were going to drop out and not pay anyway, why put him on contract in the first place? Use an EFT and get paid automatically each month. That strategy has worked for many schools and still does, but I doubt it works as well as a cash out or an agreement.

Market Realities of EFTs

1. While most drop-outs do not continue to pay, some do if they are on an agreement. You would be walking away from the money you could collect from students on agreements by not using agreements in the first place.
2. EFT is a great way to collect funds, but it's not always easy to get the student to agree to it. A person that will agree to EFT for insurance or car payments may not see martial arts lessons at the same level of necessity or security. So, as with signing a contract, a percentage of the population is uncomfortable with anyone "getting into their account." Though no one is really in their account, the perception for many is that this is risky, just like a contract.

3. In the martial arts it's tough to get hard numbers, but my experience indicates that students find it easier to quit on an EFT than on an agreement. All they have to do is tell their bank to stop making the payments. In fact, with the progress of Internet banking, many people will not sign the EFT but will insist instead on setting the payments up themselves, which gives them total cancellation control.

4. If both EFTs and agreements present problems, what's the solution? A sound cash out strategy is one solution. For ongoing payments, the combination of a 12-month agreement (for new students) with an EFT collection process, using a third-party billing company, is the best solution I have seen. Running a close second is the automatic credit card charge each month. For credit card drafts, try to get the student to use American Express, Diner's Card, or any other card that doesn't allow the holder to carry a balance.

These cards decline less, since they have to be paid off each month. AmEx may charge a little more in merchant fees but for a service business, that's a small trade-off for a more efficient collections system.

Of course, you may want to offer back-up plans such as four- or six-month cash out programs to help people who do not like EFTs or credit cards.

Billing Companies

Despite the Internet and progress with technology, collecting your own tuition is not the best use of your time and energy. Today it may seem that all you have to do is set your students up on PayPal.com or any of the many billing solutions for less than three percent. But you still have to chase declines and bounced checks.

Companies like PayPal can automate the billing, but they don't make follow-up calls or work to collect multiple months of back tuition. PayPal will attempt to collect a declined card five more days, and then it stops trying and waits until the next cycle to collect tuition. However, it won't collect the missed tuition from last month. It will collect only the current months. Students can't call PayPal to resolve billing and account issues; they have to go through the school, leaving you to handle these time-consuming matters.

This cycle can go on for months or forever unless you catch it. Then someone has to contact that student. I don't think that someone should be from your office. I think it works best when a third-party billing company makes those kinds of follow-up calls. That's why I suggest you use an industry-specific martial arts billing company instead of doing it yourself.

MATA uses Member Solutions, which is the merged company of PPS Billing and APS. PPS was run by my good friend Joe Galea and provided an excellent level of personalized service. They really did a good job hand-holding the smaller schools. APS was operated by Jeff Cohen and was probably the strongest billing company in terms of utilizing technology. The combination of the two seems like a good fit. I also use EasyPay for some of my clients. The Educational Funding Company continues to do an excellent job of tuition billing and client education. AMS has built a solid following within the Korean community.

Most billing companies charge less than eight percent for EFT and credit card debits. When considering using a billing company, the question is not how much it costs but how much more tuition can I receive for that cost?

Why Do It Yourself Billing is More Expensive

To illustrate, let's use 10 percent in total fees as an easy number on the high end for tuition billing. If you could collect $10,000 without using the billing company, but the billing company could collect the same $10,000, no more or less, you might think you have a $1,000 spread. The truth is there are many expenses involved in DIY (Do It Yourself) billing. Your own time, energy, and hard expenses associated with playing bill collector quickly eat up that $1,000 spread. Here are just some of the hard and soft expenses DIY will cost you:

1. The software to track students (including annual upgrades).
2. The mailing expenses for late notices.
3. The time to run cards, send out late notices, call late students, audit payment histories, and so on ($50,000 annual wage = $24 per hour. Double that if you are earning $100,000 per year).
4. The loss of standing with your students when you wear one hat of the wise instructor and another hat of the bill collector.
5. The loss of students. A good billing company will help you retain students by providing improved customer service and by having a stronger contractual relationship with the student.

6. The reduction in actual collections because students are not as concerned about stiffing you versus a large billing company.
7. The reduction in actual collections because you are a green belt at collections, while the billing company is a veteran black belt at getting students to pay.

What does all of this add up to? It varies with the school, of course, but I wouldn't be surprised if it were pretty close to that 10 percent mark. I give stress a high expense value. The real costs are in numbers three to five from the list above.

Playing accountant is not what you are good at, nor is it how you make your money. You will always make more by managing others than doing things yourself. A teacher nurtures, guides, and counsels students. A bill collector harasses people for money. These two roles do not mesh well. Your image as the nurturing, caring teacher can be ruined in an instant with one phone call or letter from you about missing money.

Finally, you may be a good black belt, but you are not as scary as a financial institution when it comes to deciding whom to pay. This is why big stores have their credit cards handled by outside firms. A good billing company will always collect more than you. They can be tougher than you, and it keeps you positioned in your community as a teacher, not a bill collector.

Even with the Martial Arts Teachers' Association tuition at just $24.95 a month, I use a billing company to handle it. I am a teacher by nature, and that is where I want my efforts expended. I focus on writing, editing, content creation, program development, marketing, and member retention. I enjoy all of those tasks. I do not enjoy bill collecting.

You don't hire a billing company to match your efforts. You hire them to exceed your efforts. This also allows you to focus on your core strength and responsibility as a school owner, which is creating and keeping students.

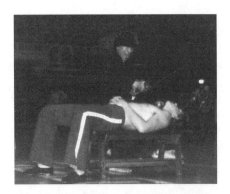

The great Hidy Ochai cuts an apple off of my throat with a sword
while blindfolded in Milan, Italy.

Who says I'm not a believer?

We had a 12-hour ride from Germany to Milan. To stay awake,
we played Led Zepplin, Genesis and YES loud for most of the
journey. I'm surprised Mr. Ochai didn't cut my head off for that.

Chapter Fourteen
How to Make Cash Outs Work

If you can keep a steady flow of new students coming in, an ideal situation is high cash outs and high monthly billing. This is being accomplished by some schools that take a somewhat unconventional approach to their cash out and upgrade strategies. This may seem to contradict my suggestion that monthly tuition is the lifeblood of the school, but it doesn't. What makes this work for the long haul is the high monthly billing. This is simply a different and somewhat riskier way of getting a high monthly cash flow and high cash outs.

It's no secret that students are at a high risk for dropping out in the first 90 days. Coming to class twice a week adds a new stress to life for a student, and it takes a little time to get in the habit. For this reason, there is a fiscal logic for attempting to cash out students during this period, because a percentage of them will stop attending anyway; and when they stop, so does your cash flow from them. The danger is in cashing out all of your new students and not having new ones coming in or a way to get the cashed-out students paying again.

Here is a strategy that works remarkably well. Again, be careful, because it can blow up in your face big time, and it has been the ruin of many schools. You can't just cash students out. You MUST work the upgrades and market for new students just as hard as the cash outs.

Cashing Out The First Program

Let's say your students join on a 12-month agreement that is $199 down and $150 per month for 11 months, which totals $1,849. That would be your base tuition with no discounts. Some students will take this offer.

You also offer a 10-percent discount for early payment, which might be five equal monthly payments of $332, which totals $1,660.

You offer a third choice, which is $1,399 in full, a $450 savings over the monthly option. This is the program you may really want your students to take and, with this kind of savings, many will. Let's compare some numbers to illustrate the pros and cons of this.

If 10 students join in a month on the standard $199 down and $150 per month program, you will get $1,990 in down payments, and your monthly cash flow technically should increase by $1,500. I say technically because no one collects 100 percent of their monthly tuition. The reality is that some students will drop out, while others will bounce their payment so, with each passing month, that $1,500 that was supposed to come to you will dwindle.

In contrast, if half of your 10 enrollments paid in full, your in-house income would be:

5 x $1,399 = $6,995

5 x $199 = $995

Total = $7,990, which is $5,991 more income

Yes, compared to the first example, your monthly cash flow is cut in half, but you weren't going to collect 100 percent of it anyway.

Look Good So Far?

It does, but, like most good things, there is a dark side. Over the course of a year of following this strategy, you may find yourself with a school full of students who have already paid for their lessons. Unless you have a way of creating new students or upgrading these paid-in-full students, you face a serious cash-flow problem.

Students who pay in advance are better leveraged to continue training than students who are paying monthly tuition. In other words, the guys who pay are the most apt to stay. So, through natural attrition, the majority of your dropouts will probably be students who did not cash out. Since your monthly cash flow is dependent on the students who are paying monthly, it will shrink with each drop out.

This is why an upgrade is so important. You want to get all of your students on a new program as soon as you can, especially those who have cashed out. This is where the Black Belt Club and Masters' Club are so critical.

Cashing Out the Second Program

By following the Black Belt Club strategies outlined in this book and on MATA, you can create a ready-made and desirable upgrade path for your students. Here are two tuition strategies for these upgrades:

Option One

Offer three choices for tuition similar to the New Student agreement outlined above. Just deduct what they have already paid in the first cash out from the new program, and use the remainder as the basis for the new payment plan.

For example, your New Student Program has a $1,399 cash out for 100 classes. The total program from white to black belt is 300 classes. That is a combination of the New Student Program (100 classes) and the Black Belt Club (200 classes). Since the student has paid for the first 100 classes, the new program will be for the remaining 200 classes. The new payments start immediately, and the time or number of classes is added to the first program.

This agreement would add the remaining time to the new program. So, if the New Student Program expires in six months (or 50 classes), your new agreement would be for 250 classes or 30 months. Payments would start right away, and this agreement would supercede or replace the current one. By upgrading now, a student can avoid future tuition increases.

Option Two

For students currently on a monthly payment program, offer Black Belt Club or Masters' Club as an upgrade for an annual fee of, say, $500, on top of their current tuition.

In the first scenario, you are getting a student who cashed out to get back on monthly tuition. In the second, you are getting a student who has not cashed out to do a small cash out of $500 to be part of the Black Belt Club.

Either way, your school is getting monthly tuition back from the students, so you are enjoying the best of both worlds: high tuition gross from new student cash outs, plus high monthly billing from the upgrades to Black Belt Club, Masters' Club, Leadership Team, etc.

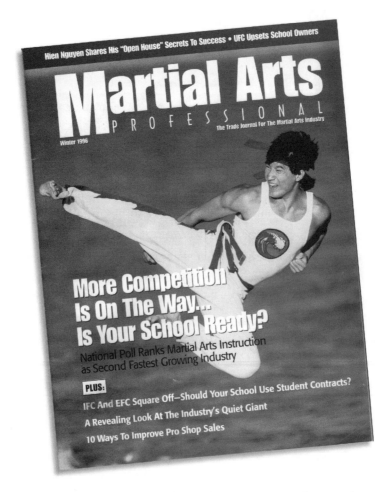

My friend Hien Nguyen on the cover of the debut issue of *Martial Arts Professional*.

I enjoyed *MAPro* more than anything else because it had such a large audience. I could have a wide impact and write provocative editorials and feature controversial subjects.

If someone complained, I always printed their letter to the editor. Sometimes I offered to return their subscription fees. Of course, since we distributed it free to the industry that was more of a subtle dig than a genuine offer.

Chapter Fifteen
How to Determine Your Retention

In consulting with school owners for more than a decade, I can pretty much predict how the initial conversations will go. I ask how many students the client wants and then how many he currently has. When he gives me his current student count (usually higher than it really is), I ask if he knows his retention. He usually says something like, "I don't think I've lost more than one or two students this year." I then ask him how many students he enrolls each month. He gives me that number (usually higher than it really is) and kind of holds his breath, waiting for a verdict on the numbers.

I quickly add the monthly enrollments together before I ask him how many students he had 12 months ago. Usually the number is just about the same as the current student count. The question then is, "Where did the students you enrolled each month for a year go?"

When I started NAPMA, I was always amazed at how many members judged the value of the service solely on how good our ad was that month. I saw message boards that proclaimed NAPMA the best service because we had the best ads. In truth, until MATA, NAPMA did have the best ads, but what's the sense of wasting money on running ads if you are going to lose the new students anyway?

Let's think of how much money and stress is put into getting new students:

1. You have to market. That costs money.

2. You have to train someone to answer the phone, or you lose the money you invested in the marketing. Eighty percent of your phone calls should set appointments to take an introductory class or trial lesson.

3. You have to confirm the appointments to make sure they show up. Eighty percent of your appointments should show up to take the intro.

4. You have to teach a trial lesson or two, and then you have to make an enrollment conference. Eighty percent of your enrollment conferences should enroll.

That is an expensive and stressful process to go through. But, if you do it well, 50 percent of the people who call you will give you money. If you do it poorly, and most do, far less than 50 percent will give you money.

This is why retention is so critical. Once students are in your school, it is far easier to service and sell them than to have to repeat this process. Imagine the nightmare if the only way to get paid was to go through that process for each student's monthly tuition. The beauty of the membership-based business is that, if you do a good job of teaching and servicing your students, they will continue to pay, month in and month out. This is why improving retention is mission one in turning a school around. Lazy school owners want a magic ad to fill their school, when in truth they need better classroom management to keep their students in class.

The Formula for Retention

The first step toward improving retention is to find a way to measure it. Here's a simple formula to help determine your retention throughout the year:

("Active students" are those who have attended in the past two weeks).

1. Start with the total number of active students as of December 31 last year.
2. Add to that the total number of new students who have enrolled year-to-date.
3. Count the number of active students you currently have.

Divide #3 above by the sum of #1 & #2. That is your retention rate as a percentage.

For example, if you were to do this in April:

1. December 31 ends with 150 students
2. New students January 1 to April 30 = 40 @ 10 per month
3. 150 + 40 = 190 students (this is 100-percent retention)
4. Current active count = 165 students
5. 165 ÷ 190 = .86 or 86-percent retention

The shorter the period of time, the higher the percentage. Don't be fooled into thinking you have an 86-percent retention rate year round with these figures. Most schools end up with around 50 percent for the year. You, of course, want to push it as high as you can but it has to be more than 50 percent to grow.

The Truth About the Martial Arts Business

The NAPMA booth at an early seminar. That's my brother Jim on the right in his classic Secret Service fig-leaf pose. Notice no one is on his side?

On the backdrop, you can see the jump side kick ad I describe in The Core Dynamics chapter on Black Belt Eyes.

Chapter Sixteen
How to Improve Renewals and Retention

The Black Belt Club, Black Sash Club, or Bushido Club

The Black Belt Club (BBC), Black Sash Club (BSC) or Bushido Club (BC) have nothing to do with selling belts or promising students they will get a black belt.

The BBC goes right to the Core Dynamic of Valuing What You Do (again). You are a very special professional in your town. You have worked very hard and endured significant hardship to earn your rank and position. You have a lot to teach people in this community. That's why, if you Value What You Do, you will do everything you can to teach only people who are serious about learning and are committed to earning their black belt.

That's what the BBC is all about. You enroll a student in a 12-month New Student membership to give him a chance to evaluate your school and the martial arts. It also gives you a chance to make sure the student will be a good fit in your school. Believe me, when you start thinking and operating this way, you will end up firing some students/parents.

In those early stages, your job is to help them understand that, whatever their goal in the martial arts or in life, the ultimate realization of that goal is in earning a black belt. You train people to black belt and beyond. That is what you do.

Don't train people until green belt if you can help it... and you can help it with a good Black Belt Club. It makes no sense for you – as someone who truly values what he or she does – to waste your time, energy, and spirit on a student who is only going to train until football or swimming season starts. Your job is to inspire the desire to earn a black belt.

Early on, equate everything good with a black belt. Let's line up like black belts, gang! How does a black belt punch? Wrist bent or wrist straight? How would a black belt sit in your school and listen to the teacher?

The goal is to create a system that monitors your student's progress and goals so that you know exactly when they are ready to make the commitment to earn a black belt. In your school, that is represented by membership in the BBC.

Tying the BBC Progress and Goals Into Exams

Before your student's first exam, require the following survey to be turned in the week before the test. This will clearly indicate where a student is in his progress toward earning a black belt. The Student Progress and Goals Survey is great for targeting students for renewals.

Student Progress and Goals Survey

1. *Why did you originally enroll in martial arts?* This tells you what the student is seeking. You want to make sure you are providing this. If he says "self defense," but you spend all of your white belt classes on forms, you may be in trouble with this student.

2. *In what ways has the program helped you so far?* This is not only for you, but it's always good to have students stop and think about how they are benefiting. This also tells you what kind of job you are doing. An enthused answer could be a signal he is ready for BBC. A less than enthusiastic answer could mean you still have work to do.

3. *What are your long-term goals with the program?* Of course, we want to see "black belt" here, but we may be surprised to see "to teach" or "green belt."

4. *What steps are you willing to take to achieve your goals with the program?* "BBC" is what we'd like to see here, along with "train hard" and "don't miss class."

5. *Please write down three serious goals and what you are going to do to accomplish them.* This is a helpful exercise for anyone. "Black belt" is an answer that tells us this student may be ready for BBC.

Review the survey results and schedule an appointment for the most qualified A-students for a BBC presentation.

Launch Your BBC in Three Steps

I suggest you have your first color belt exam for a new student within the first six weeks. Get color around a student's waist as soon as you can, so they can feel that they have made some progress. I use the gold belt as the first belt instead of yellow. Yellow is associated with fear and cowardice, while gold is something we all want.

The three-step cycle of creating BBC students works in conjunction with the exam cycle. Our goal is to find students who are highly qualified to join the BBC, which means:

1. They have black belt as a goal.
2. They are willing to train at your school to earn that black belt.
3. They have the support of their family for this goal.
4. They are ready and willing to pay additional tuition for membership in the BBC.

The key is that, when you sit down in a BBC conference, you want to know that this person is fully qualified. You don't want to make a BBC presentation and then hope you're talking to the right person. There are two reasons for this.

1. You want to present your BBC as being a prestigious club that students can get into only with their instructor's recommendation. If you offer the BBC to unqualified students, you give the impression you are desperate.
2. Students who are not yet ready for the BBC know they are not. Everyone knows what the requirements are, because a good BBC is highly visible within the school. Making a more expensive tuition presentation to a student who is not qualified creates tension and can deteriorate your relationship with the student.

Unlike the prosecution in the O.J. Simpson trial, you want to make sure the glove fits before you ask them to try it on.

Step One

Every Monday or at least once a week, go through all your student attendance cards with your staff. Briefly discuss each student with your team. How is he doing? Why has she been missing class? Rate each student with A, B, or C.

A. A-rated students are like us. They really enjoy the martial arts, they don't miss class, and they have a great attitude.
B. B-rated students are good students but are not as visibly enthused as the A students. They may come to some special events, but not all. Their attitude may be good but a bit inconsistent.
C. C-rated students seem to be less motivated. They come to class less than they need to in

order to progress, and they seldom, if ever, come to special events. These students are at the highest risk for dropping out.

By the end of the rating you will have three piles of cards. Target your C students for private lessons or extra attention, to prevent them from dropping out. Target A students for potential BBC presentation appointments.

Step Two

When you get the Student Progress and Goals Sheets back, look for students who have set black belt as their goal. Match those students to your A pile. A-rated students who have set black belt as a goal are prime candidates and usually are quick to upgrade their program to BBC. B- and C-rated students who turn in a Progress and Goal sheet with black belt listed as a goal need to be carefully considered before receiving a BBC presentation.

Many people set goals they have no real intention of following through on. These goals are often more of a wish than a goal. We all have a goal of being rich but, if we're not willing to do the work to become rich, then it's just a wish. This is not to say a B or C student would never upgrade to BBC. It just means your odds are less with them, and their joining could water down the prestige of the program. I suggest you stay focused on your A students for BBC presentations.

Step Three

Set appointments with students for presentation of the BBC membership. A good example of a BBC presentation is on my CD and DVD, *The Black Belt Club Upgrade*. I show a BBC presentation, then replay it and stop the tape to explain why I asked certain questions the way I did and how I overcame the price objections. You can get a copy in the MATA Store.

The book that started it all. *Black Belt Management* sold more than 1,000 copies at $100+ and was the catalyst to NAPMA.

The book still sells well to this day and is in its fourth edition.

Chapter Seventeen
Curriculum Design:
The Recipe Book for Your School

I had lunch recently with a fourth dan in Uechi Ryu. We talked about how the Eastern mind-set is so different from the Western, and the confusion that creates for many instructors. Culturally, the East is more about conformity, or as I call it, cloning, than the West, where rugged individualism and innovation are instilled.

This prompted him to tell me a story of the greatest fighter in his system. This was a Japanese fellow who, as a young man, went to his uncle to learn karate. The uncle turned him away, but the guy kept returning. Finally, the uncle took him but made him clean the school, wash the toilets, and generally play the role of school janitor for a year or so before teaching him any karate.

When he felt the student was ready, he took him to other schools where he would get the heck beat out of him. Sometimes American GIs would come into the school to spar, and the uncle would have them fight his nephew, who got pounded. This lasted years, until finally the nephew began to win some of the fights. Eventually, he won them all.

The guy told me this with pride and added you just don't see that level of dedication anymore. I said, "Of course not. That's a stupid way to teach." He was shocked. That is one of those stories instructors tell students to inspire them. And, as usual, the student doesn't question it. I can't help but be curious as to why someone would teach that way.

My comment to him was here you had someone with this kind of talent and potential, and you risked losing him by making him clean toilets for a year and then have him get beat up. That's just dumb. That guy could have been a great martial artist years before he finally reached his potential. Luckily, he stuck it out, but who knows how many others with similar potential dropped out due to such an insane program? The instructor may have been a great master, but his curriculum was nuts, even if it does make a nice story.

If there is any area of your program you will want to scrutinize mercilessly, it should be your curriculum. As a good restaurant has a book of unique recipes, your curriculum is your school's recipe book. Most of us either inherit the curriculum we came up in or we join an organization and adopt their curriculum. Because of the Eastern roots of martial arts, there is an inherent bias towards conforming to existing methods. This, in time, leads to a one-size-fits-all approach to martial arts.

The Masters on Change

Here are some quotations regarding styles from three of the most influential martial artists in history:

"There are no styles in karate." – Gichin Funakoshi

"You limit a style by labeling it." – Bruce Lee

"The style serves the student. The student doesn't serve the style." – Joe Lewis

Despite my roots in tae kwon do, my responsibility is to my students, not tae kwon do, kickboxing, Joe Lewis Fighting Systems, or any other source of information. My job is to create the best black belts possible in a school that authentically represents what I believe in. In large part, that responsibility is expressed through my curriculum.

When Does a System Freeze?

The history of the arts, however, is the tendency to freeze a curriculum and then resist any change or suggestion of change. I love Shotokan and know that the reason I did so well in forms division was my adaptation of the core elements of Shotokan, which is deeper balance and more powerful and crisp blocks and punches than my root system of tae kwon do.

We have the great system of Shotokan because of the work of Gichin Funakoshi. In fact, the genesis of Shotokan is in the massive change Funakoshi's made to Okinawan karate. He radically changed the recipe book, yet for the most part the book has not changed since.

It's also entertaining to me to see modern jeet kune do teachers argue over what is real JKD. If anyone didn't want his system to freeze, it was Bruce Lee. He was way ahead of his time in his approach to creating a practical martial art that was not confined or restricted by history.

Joe Lewis is someone who has continually updated his material. Recently we trained one-on-one for the first time in over a decade. He had me fire some of the excellent Joe Lewis Fighting Systems' combinations on the bag in my garage. He stopped me and started to show me how to throw a straight right hand. My mouth kind of dropped, my eyes got wide, and I shook my head in disbelief. He said, "What?" I said, "That is the exact opposite of what you taught me in the 80s!" He said, "What? I'm not supposed to evolve?" It was the perfect response.

Here was a 60-year-old black belt who was in his fourth decade as a worldwide recognized pioneer and superstar, but in his mind, he is in his fourth decade of evolution. While I'm on the subject of Joe Lewis, let me also mention this. Joe is a very traditional martial artist. I am, too. We don't express our traditions by holding on to techniques or rituals. We express them by making sure our students: execute with proper form, can defend themselves and develop the tenacity to never quit.

Can You Teach Confidence?

Schools today talk a lot about teaching confidence. They have words of the week and life skills training, which is great. I wish my instructors had taught me about goal setting when I was a kid. But I don't think confidence can be taught. It's too experiential and situational. I do think schools can present experiences that will help students to gain self-confidence.

For instance, Joe Lewis taught me that confidence as a fighter comes when you are hurt and/or exhausted, not when you are fresh. When you learn to stay dangerous despite being at a disadvantage, your confidence builds. Confidence comes from experiencing those times that even though you may not win the fight, you can survive it. That translates to all areas of life and has helped me tremendously.

But it wasn't Lewis' saying that to me that taught it to me. His saying it to me helped me understand the process, but the process is what taught it to me. The process was years of full-contact sparring with him in a 12-foot ring in the Florida heat with no air conditioning. There were times he hit me so hard the room changed colors. But I never went down, never quit, and never missed a workout (you can see a video of him knocking the wind out of me in the *Truth About the Martial Arts Business* section of MartialArtsTeachers.com).

Regardless of your background and what techniques you were taught, what are the principles of martial arts that are important to you? How do you want to express them in your curriculum? How can you create a recipe that instills those principles in a dish that keeps the students coming back for more?

For me, the principles were respect; tenacity; technical execution to honor the arts; the ability to defend yourself against nine out of ten people your size; physical conditioning; and the attitude of resilient optimism.

Core Lessons I Wanted My Curriculum to Teach

1. Respect

My school was based upon ideals of respect and courtesy. We expressed this in many ways, from how we addressed each other to how we bowed in and out of class.

2. Tenacity

The never-quit attitude is critical to gaining self confidence. You're tired? Rest when you get home. You're banged up? You're breaking my heart. Pain is part of the training.

3. Technical Execution to Honor the Arts

We honor the rich history of the martial arts by working as hard as we can to execute the techniques as well as possible. Acceptance of a sloppy side kick is like an exhibit of a sloppy painting in a museum. We work to honor the arts by constantly working to improve the quality and efficacy of our techniques.

4. Self Defense

The martial arts are fighting arts. To me, the principle is peace through superior firepower. We never abuse what we've learned, but if we need to write the check, we have the money in the bank. This is also why I introduced Bill Kipp, Peyton Quinn, CDT, and Krav Maga to the industry at my NAPMA World Conferences. These guys were the leaders in realistic self defense, and I knew that many instructors, like me, were limited to our own styles' ideas of self defense. Though I was limited, that didn't mean it was not important to me.

5. Physical Conditioning

Using the Phase 1 – 3 methods of teaching, we were able to make sure that our black belts were in excellent shape (learn more about phase 1 – 3 in *Black Belt Management* or MartialArtsTeachers.com).

6. Resilient Optimism

This is the attitude that if you work hard in a smart direction, good things will happen. It's the idea that if you do good things, good things come back to you. It's a resilient optimism that if you work hard and stay positive, things will work out better than if you didn't. Rather than saying to yourself, "What did I do wrong?" we say, "What will I do better next time?" Now that we have the principles that are important to me to teach, how can I use my curriculum to instill them in my student body?

Let's take a look at the evolution of my own system. My hope is that this will help you to update your own.

When I opened my school, I presented the exact curriculum that I was raised on (figure 1 on the next page).

Among the many problems that created for me was that I had a lot more kids in my school than my instructors did. Martial arts forms, hyungs, or kata were designed by highly disciplined adults to be taught to other highly disciplined adults in a military atmosphere. They were not designed to be taught to an eight-year-old kid.

Teaching kids traditional forms, especially multiple forms, can be very difficult for everyone involved. This is not to say that forms don't have value, but your curriculum is how you package the forms. Going back to the recipe analogy, a good curriculum is like a healthy, tasty, enriching meal that you look forward to, while a poorly designed one is as attractive as a plate full of broccoli to the average kid. It's good for you, but it's hard to get down.

If you look at the curriculum in figure 1, we can see some common problems:

1. The program is front loaded. It has far more requirements in the early ranks than in the advanced ranks. Typically, this overwhelms white belts and bores brown and black belts. This is a classic pyramid curriculum. The majority of the material is at the lower levels, and it tapers off as the student moves up in rank. We prefer to see more of an even column pattern. This lessens the amount of material required for the new student, which means they will have more time to improve on fewer techniques. This gives the student a higher sense of competence, and competence leads to confidence. When someone feels they are "getting it" in the early stages, they develop a momentum that keeps them coming to class. When they feel they are not "getting it" or not very good at it, they find excuses not to continue. Have you ever had a student drop out and tell you that he or she is too much of a perfectionist to continue? This is a student who takes pride in doing things right, but your recipe made it too hard, so they quit.

2. The focus is almost 100-percent traditional material. Traditional material is not immediately practical enough to hold the interest of the modern student. I like to give students, especially new students, material they feel they can use right away. When a new student joins your school to learn self defense, and in the first class you spend most of the time on front stance, down block, and horse stance punching, that student may not see the *instant value* they were looking for. The sooner the student feels they have something they can

Figure 1

White to Orange (four months)
Traditional Karate
1. Down block-Lunge punch
2. High block
3. Forearm block
4. Side block
5. Reverse advance
6. Knifehand block
7. Front stance
8. Back stance
9. Horse stance

Strikes
1. Front kick
2. Back kick
3. Side kick
4. Round kick
5. Backfist
6. Reverse punch

Traditional form – Chonji

Orange to Green (four months)
Strikes
1. Low – High kick
2. Spin back kick
3. Jump front Kick

Six one steps
Two forms – Tan Gun & Pyungdan Shodan
Free sparring

Green to Blue
Strikes
1. Hook kick
2. Jump round kick
3. Jump side kick

Six one steps
Two forms – To San & Pyungdan Nidan

Two-on-one sparring

Blue to Fourth Brown
Strikes
1. Jump spin back kick
2. Crescent kick

Six one steps
Multiple sparring

Board Breaks
1. Round kick - two boards
2. Reverse punch - two boards (women could use a palm heel)
3. Running jump side kick over two people – three boards

Two forms – Won Hyo & Pyungdan Samdan

Fourth Brown to Third Brown
Two forms – Tai Gyi & Pyungdan Sadan
Three creative* one steps

Two creative board breaks

Third Brown to Second Brown
Two forms – Hwarang & Pyungdan Odan
Three creative one steps

Two creative board breaks

Second Degree to First Brown
Two forms – Chogi & Chung Moo
Three creative one steps
Two creative board breaks

First Brown to First Black Belt
Two forms – Batsai & Kwan Gae
Three creative one steps
Two creative board breaks

*Creative means the students make it up.

Figure 2

White to Gold (two months)

Blocks
1. Left cover
2. Right cover
3. Left trap
4. Right trap
5. Left down sweep
6. Right down sweep

Strikes
1. Front kick
2. Back kick
3. Jab
4. Reverse punch
5. Elbow #1
6. Elbow #2

Gold to Orange

Strikes
1. Front leg round kick
2. Side kick
3. Hook punch
4. Uppercut
5. Elbow #3
6. Elbow #4

Combinations 1 - 3
Fighting Form

Orange to Green

Strikes
1. Low-high kick
2. Spin back kick
3. Jump front kick

Traditional Karate
1. Front stance
2. Back stance
3. Down block
4. High block
5. Side block

Sparring – blocking contact only

Green to Blue

Strikes
1. Hook kick
2. Jump round kick
3. Jump side kick

Traditional Karate
1. Forearm block
2. Knifehand block
3. Reverse advance

Sparring – body contact only

Blue to Fourth Brown

Traditional form – Tosan

Strikes
Jump spin back kick

Sparring – light contact kickboxing

Fourth Brown to Third Brown

Traditional form – Tai Gyi

Three kumites (traditional combinations)

Sparring – light contact kickboxing

Third Brown to Second Brown

Traditional form – Hwarang
Three creative kumites

Second Brown to First Brown

Traditional form – Chung Moo
Three creative kumites

First Brown to First Black Belt

Traditional form – Kwan gae
Three creative kumites

Note: You can see much of this curriculum demonstrated at MartialArtsTeachers.com use, the sooner he or she feels value in the effort. Too often, we start with techniques that are theory-based rather than reality-based. We end up saying things like, "You would never really block this way, but..."

3. People like to do what they are good at, and traditional martial arts are hard to learn. This is not to say you should drop your traditional material, but rather rework the recipe.

4. There are far more forms than necessary. Remember, it was not uncommon for a traditional instructor in the East to teach only one form. Everything in class was built around that form. This curriculum requires 17 forms for black belt. Some ranks required three forms. That is simply too much for the average student to master. Three forms in one belt cycle is not reasonable or productive.

Let me walk you through the processes that I went through to change the recipe. At first, it's not easy to make wholesale changes to your program. As we saw in The Core Dynamic, The Control Factor, we have a strong connection to many of these techniques and forms. However, once you begin the process of improving the recipes, it becomes exciting. This is also an important step towards Finding Your Own Voice. Question everything you teach and have been taught from the little stories we tell to the longest form. Take your artist hat off and put on your lab coat.

What Do I Want to Accomplish with This Program?
My First Changes to the Curriculum

Note: You can see video clips of many of these descriptions in *The Truth About the Martial Arts Business* section of MartialArtsTeachers.com

My first step was reducing the number of forms. I asked myself, what does this form teach? Maybe, like Yul Kok, it had difficult combinations on each side that taught complex ambidextrous motion. Is there another form at the level that does a better or worse job of creating bilateral coordination? I'd drop one of them. Maybe there is a very basic form, like Chonji, that doesn't bring anything to the table except making the life of a white belt and white belt instructor more frustrating. I dropped it. After walking through this process, I reduced 17 forms to eight.

Next, I looked at our board breaking. I was so tired of watching students bounce off boards that I dropped board breaking for all ranks except black belt exams. Instead, I created a quarterly Board Breaking Seminar where I charged the students to take a one-hour seminar on how to break boards. This turned a highly stressful aspect of the exam process that cost us money in dropouts into a highly profitable and fun special event that improved retention.

I also pushed multiple sparring back until brown belt.

Keep in mind that you can always teach students something you feel is important, but you don't have to make it a requirement for rank. New school owners usually try to make everything a requirement because they want to create super students. That's a good attitude with a flawed approach.

The less you require on exams, the higher the quality of execution. Plus, since you have fewer requirements to cover in class, you have more time to be creative and work on techniques, combinations, creative forms, etc. that you feel are important but not requirements.

For instance, a jump spinning crescent kick is a fun and very hard kick to execute. If you require it at a specific rank, then a percentage of your students will be able to perform it adequately, but many will not. It's a difficult kick that requires jumping and flexibility, and some students will get nauseated from the spinning. This is especially true of students in the 30+ age group.

Ask yourself, how important is this kick? Well, I think it's a skill I want my students to have. Fair enough. How about if you teach it and practice it in class but don't require it? Then it's a fun challenge for the students but not a potential obstacle to their advancement. You have the best of both worlds. The students who can perform this will, and those who would never use it after being shown it won't have the concern that this may hinder their progress.

Round Two
Less Yak – More Smack

After a year or so, we noticed an improvement in quality and retention. Also, classes were easier to teach and manage because we didn't have so many requirements. Still, I felt we were requiring more traditional material than I felt valuable this early in a student's journey. Despite my love of forms, I want my students to be able to fight first and foremost. Requiring the six basic blocks, four kicks, and three stances from white belt to orange belt was not giving my students the practical material I wanted them to have.

White to Gold Belt

As part of the solution, we inserted gold belt between white and orange. From white to gold took six to eight weeks, and the requirements changed dramatically.

We dropped all traditional blocks and stances and replaced them with kickboxing skills. Instead of six traditional blocks, we had six fighting blocks.

1. Left cover
2. Right cover
3. Left trap
4. Right trap
5. Left down sweep
6. Right down sweep

These blocks were easy to learn, highly practical, and easy to work into drills. They gave the student *instant value*.

For strikes, white to gold belts also learned:

1. Front kick
2. Back kick
3. Jab
4. Reverse punch (cross), which is very easy to feel competent at early.
5. Elbow #1
6. Elbow #2

Though this is actually an increase in strikes, they were much easier to learn than traditional blocks. So we were able to accomplish more in less time.

Gold to Orange Belt

The requirements from gold to orange also changed. Rather than teach the back leg round kick, as we had before, we taught the front leg round kick. This was much easier to learn and work into drills and combinations. We kept side kick at this rank but thought hard about moving it to orange belt. The back leg round kick was moved to orange belt.

Kicks:

1. Front leg round kick

2. Side kick

The strikes from Gold to Orange were

Hand strikes:

1. Hook punch

2. Uppercut

3. Elbow #3

4. Elbow #4

We took the kicks and strikes they had been taught and created three required Fighting Combinations.

1. Step finger jab to the eyes (jab with fist for kids) – step up side kick to the knee/legs – elbow #2 to the head.

2. Step in jab – reverse punch – clearing front leg front kick

3. Skip in front leg round kick – jab-reverse punch-hook punch – clearing round kick (weight shifts back from hook punch as student fires a front leg round kick)

Students enjoy these combinations. Once you demonstrate them and show how effective these strikes can be, the students are excited to execute them with full force in the mirror and on targets. You can see in their eyes that they feel powerful. That is a very different look than before when we had them walking up and down the floor doing basics.

We took these three Fighting Combinations and linked them into a pattern to create Fighting Form One. This was an easy form to teach and learn. It was an excellent replacement for Chonji.

This also allowed us to spend more time in class doing pad drills, relationship (distance and alignment) drills, and defensive drills. These changes provided three immediate benefits to the students:

1. Students felt an Instant Value in the class that is hard to get teaching traditional basics such as front stance down block-lunge punch.

2. The drills made the class more interactive, which added energy to the class. It also facili-

tated students' meeting each other and bonding, as we would have them introduce themselves to their partner before each drill.

3. The drills pushed the students, which helped their conditioning faster than walking through traditional basics did. Often, a traditional white belt class barely breaks a sweat, as the techniques require detailed explanations and then slow execution. Our new mantra was, "Less yak; more smack," and it worked.

4. The defensive drills helped prepare students for sparring. Not only do many students need to learn how to deal with someone hitting or striking at them, they also have to learn how to hit someone. Have you ever seen a student, usually a female adult, do a drill and tap her partner with a punch and then reach out and say, "I'm so sorry…"? For the past 20 years or so, the "don't ever hit someone" message has been drilled into a large portion of our population. Smart relationship and defensive drills really help you overcome this for your new students. (You can see these drills in the Video department of MartialArtsTeachers. com or SparringDrills.com)

Retention was much higher as a result of these changes. Equally important, the principles that were important to me were now being expressed more clearly and directly in my school as a result of these changes.

Tradition is an attitude, it's not a technique.

The WAKO USA Team - from left to right, Jerry Rhome, John Longstreet, Brian Dorsey, Troy Dorsey, Ray McCallum, and me - at the infamous Checkpoint Charlie at the Berlin Wall.

Once we got in, only John Longstreet and I were adventurous enough to get on a train and explore.

Within months, the wall came down. We take full credit.

Summary
A School Full of Pooh Bears

There is a great line attributed to Winston Churchill that 'if you are in your 20s and are not a Liberal, you don't have a heart. If you are in your 40s and not a Conservative, you don't have a brain.' While I'm not agreeing or disagreeing with him, his message relates clearly to how your belief system can change at different stages of your life and career.

Many of us went from the dungeon dojo to a more motivational school with a big emphasis on personal development. This attracted a huge kids' market, but did it create better martial artists? I don't think so. It's pretty clear I'm not the only one, because we are seeing a return to a more adult-oriented and intense school, but not a return to the dungeon days of past.

The first time I visited New York City, I got into an argument with a black belt who was my host for the weekend in his small townhouse outside the Bronx. It was 1992, and I was in the midst of a transition for my school from a school of adult fighters to a school of kids, with an emphasis on positive development.

The argument rose from a conversation we had concerning his three-year-old son. I asked if he planned to have his kid take martial arts lessons. He made it clear that his son would learn to defend himself. I added that the martial arts are also really good for character development. The line had been drawn in the sand. He said he didn't care about his kid "helping old ladies across the road." He wanted his kid to be able to "knock someone on their ass" if needed.

I regurgitated a line that I had heard at a seminar that, "The world didn't need more fighters, it needed more respect and courtesy." He scoffed at the notion. He said his kid gets plenty of good messages from his favorite TV shows like *Sesame Street*. The boy attended church each Sunday with his mom and attended a good school. All of them taught him to be respectful and polite. What they didn't teach him was how to get out of a fight. He wanted his boy to be able to handle himself. I told him his approach to martial arts was "old-school thinking." He laughed, and we agreed to disagree.

Now, over a decade later, not only am I a dad, but I've also watched the martial arts evolve from a unique, cross-style vantage point. The more I think about it, the more I believe that my foul-mouthed friend was right, with some qualifications.

The Motivational Daycare Center

I certainly don't feel that the movement towards character development has been bad for schools; it has been great. However, years ago I warned that if we continued to stray away from our core services and values, our schools would become little more than motivational day care centers. I think we are getting pretty close.

The life-skills programs in schools too often are there for one reason; to overcome the concerns of the mothers of the kids in class. Most dads want their kid to be honest and respectful, but dads tend to understand the value of being able to deal with bullies and life's physical threats more than most moms.

There are many students who come to us from bad situations where they have few if any role models of good behavior, and this is where the martial arts school can shine. Still, I think that child will be influenced more by a powerful black belt conducting himself or herself in a respectful manner and not abusing his power than the reciting of a sterile end-of-class story about the tortoise and the hare.

In traditional martial arts, respect is a word that is emphasized from day one. The belts work as a great goal-setting program and, certainly, developing a never-quit attitude is key to moving through the ranks.

To be clear, I see nothing wrong with organizing the lessons of martial arts into life skills to make sure they are articulated and apparent to the students and their families. That is like spice on the meal; it is not the meal.

Today it seems that instructors are focused more on their ability to get kids to recite pledges of good behavior and scream "YES SIR" than on their students' capacity to "knock someone on their duffs" if they need to.

I know an excellent black belt who has transformed his school from adults to kids and now back to adults again. Like me, he had marketed to kids and cloned what the "Big Schools" were

The Truth About the
Martial Arts Business

doing for character development. He began to pass kids for their "effort" in order to save their "self esteem." More and more he found his school had become a kids' center with hundreds of children yelling "YES, SIR!" at all the right moments during a speech.

Never mind that many of the kids really didn't know what they were responding to. They just knew at the end of a question to scream "YES, SIR!" He also noticed that his upper-ranks began to look pretty weak. His exams became celebrations of mediocrity with lots of smiles, high fives, and weak technical skills. While passing every kid in exams may be good for retention, that very fact means eventually you are going to have a school full of Pooh Bears. Kids who are soft and nice, but easy targets, despite the color of the belt.

In time, my friend began to dislike his own school. He didn't want to be there. He missed the camaraderie and pride of creating black belts to whom he could teach fighting, without upsetting the student's mommy.

There's No Crying as a Black Belt!

Then one day, a threshold event occurred that left him disgusted and ready to make some serious changes. One of his 11-year-old Pooh Bears came running into the school, bleeding and crying. It seems another kid, who was no bigger or older, had popped him in the nose. The student had been standing in front of his karate school, wearing his uniform and his BLACK BELT while waiting for his parents. Somehow he got into an exchange of words with a neighborhood kid who punched or slapped him in the nose.

My friend was sickened. Not only had an unfortunate incident happened in front of his school, but one of his black belts was crying and bleeding. To paraphrase Tom Hanks in the movie *A League of Their Own*, "there's no crying as a black belt!"

My friend was humiliated. That's not supposed to happen. When we were students, stories of our school's black belts defending themselves always ended with the bad guy in the hospital. That event was the catalyst for the end of the student creed and passing exams for merely making the effort to show up. It has taken him two years, but he now is back to nearly as many active students, with only 20 percent under the age of 12 – a complete reversal of where he had been when the kid got popped.

He looks forward to going to his school each night and is enjoying running the school with a healthy mixture of personal development and realistic training and expectations.

My friend is one of the best black belts I know. He and I have talked about this new dynamic in the industry dozens of times. The conclusion that I've come to is that the introduction into the classroom of positive character development is a good "undercurrent" for a school. It's the perfect counter-balance to good physical training and self defense.

But many schools are out of balance. The line that, "We don't just teach punching and kicking..." has become a cop out for not teaching strong core self defense and technical skills. Don't apologize for teaching punching and kicking (or grappling).

Technical execution and self defense have become an afterthought to personal development. Why? It's a heck of a lot easier to teach a kid to act like a Boy Scout with a belt than to take the time, effort, and honesty required to produce a black belt who can defend himself or herself.

But, as many people have discovered, in time you may be teaching at a school you hardly recognize. You will have students who stand up straight when shaking hands during their "polite greetings" but who have rubber backbones.

It's important to be OK with the fact that martial arts can't be all things to all people. The very term martial means military. Military relates to matters of war. This doesn't mean each class is devoted to killing or war tactics; it means that our foundation is one of peace through superior firepower. It's a program of self worth that starts with the concept that:

'I am worth protecting. No one will touch me without my permission.'

In a good program, as your skills improve, your sense of contribution, respect, and responsibility increases as well. Today, we're seeing hybrid black belts awarded for blindfolding themselves so they can know what it's like to be blind or spending a day in a wheelchair. This seems more like a high school sociology class than a study in the martial arts. To me, the ultimate black belt is a noble warrior who uses the martial arts as a method of personal and physical growth. It is a very individual pursuit that is better taken eyes wide open than blindfolded.

These are core attitudes and benefits that were inherent in the arts long before any student creed or message of the week.

I thought this was an appropriate shot to finish with. *The Truth About the Martial Arts Business* represents a long path for me from Florida karate jock to The Martial Arts Teachers' Association.

I thank you for taking the time to read about it.
I hope you find it helpful and enjoyed it as much as I did.

I always like letters from readers, so please drop me
a line at johngraden@martialartsteachers.com.

I also hope to see you as a member of the Martial Arts Teachers' Association at
MartialArtsTeachers.com

Keep kicking,

John Graden

Appendix I
Is Owning a School Right For You?
Are You Right for Owning a School?

Iknew from my first night in white belt class on February 12, 1974, at age 13, that I was going to do martial arts for the rest of my life. I was teaching professionally by age 16 and have been teaching ever since. However, I never wanted to own a school, at least until the mid-1980s when I was in my twenties.

For one thing, I had no business experience. For that matter, I hadn't even finished high school. Second, I was not money directed. I was far more focused on quality of life, and in your twenties, it doesn't take much money to have the lifestyle you want. I slept until 10 a.m., ran three to five miles on the beach, trained at the school, took a nap, and then taught for a few hours. It was the life of a karate bum and I loved it.

Mike Anderson, the co-founder of the PKA (Professional Karate Association) and WAKO (World Association of KickBoxing Organizations) tried to persuade me to open a school in the early 1980s. He, along with Fred Wren, had operated some very successful schools in the St. Louis area. He tried to tell me I could do the same thing, but I had no clue of how to run a school. I knew I could teach well, but that was about it.

In 1984, Joe Lewis convinced me to open my first school. Before that, we trained and sparred together at the various locations around town where I taught my classes. One day we were on a basketball court, the next day in a college fitness facility, and another at a boxing club. Joe noticed that I was building a solid core of excellent students who would follow me from location to location to take afternoon and evening classes. Kathy Marlor, Phil Beatty, Kevin Walker of Project Action, Kim Cox, my brother Mark, and eventually even action movie star Gary Daniels (who came to me already as an excellent black belt) all were training hard in my classes almost daily.

The day Joe called me on the phone it was a seminal moment in my life. I was in the kitchen of my rented house when I heard him say, "You need to give your students a home. You need to give them a place they can take pride in." That hit home. Mike Anderson's promise of making good money never struck a chord with me, but I certainly could relate to having pride in your school. Since I had often slept at my school when I was a kid, I understood totally the idea of creating a home for my students. I started looking for a location the next day.

Martial arts is not an ordinary business. Because there is no educational requisite to open a school, schools are opened by people on many levels of experience and skill. You can come out of college with an MBA and open a school. You can also come right out of prison and open a school. There are no hard standards or requirements. Some have what it takes and some do not, regardless of what system they study.

How can you find out where you stand? I've created a measuring tool to help you, whether you are considering opening a school or you own a school and need perspective on your role. You will discover if owning a school is for you, or if you are the right person to own a school. Most of us launch our school with dreams of influencing hundreds of students. As the Core Dynamic of Clarity of Purpose illustrates, that is not enough to make a school grow.

This questionnaire covers 100 key points in 10 categories. It is not scientific, but it is helpful and, according to the guys I tested it on, very powerful.

The Truth About the
Martial Arts Business

Martial Arts School Owner Preparation Questionnaire

Answer each question with Yes or No. Score yourself one point for each YES.

There are 10 categories of questions. Of course, there could be more categories and questions, but these questions will stimulate your thinking, helping you to make a good decision.

1. Preparation and Timing
2. Your Leadership Skills
3. Strategic Planning
4. Sales Strategies and Tactics
5. Systems for Student Service
6. Profitability Timeline
7. Your School as a Success
8. The Key Numbers and Assets
9. The Core Dynamics
10. Are You the Right Person for the Job?

A. Preparation and Timing

a.   I have been using the systems I will implement for at least six months.

b.   My family, attorney, CPA, and mentors are behind this idea.

c.   I understand that I am not selling my style or my credentials. I am selling benefits and results for my students.

d.   My school will have low overhead, but I am positioned to expand should I need to.

e.   I am in excellent physical shape.

f.   My martial arts skills are the best of anyone in the school I learned in.

g.   I have at least six months of expenses in savings.

h.   I have been teaching and improving my teaching skills for at least a year.

i.   I have researched the area and have calculated my Pull Radius and Potential Ratio.

j.   My space matches my rent, and both match my area. I can see myself grossing ten times my monthly rent within the first year.

B. Leadership Skills

a. I would rather lead than follow in most situations.

b. I am comfortable directing, challenging, and encouraging students and potential staff.

c. I do not put off confrontation even if the situation is uncomfortable.

d. I would rather fail and correct than not try something new I feel will help.

e. I am an expert in martial arts, but I will always have much to learn and am seeking knowledge each day.

f. I understand that my expertise in martial arts does not make me an expert in life.

g. People tend to look to me for direction in many different situations.

h. I respect suggestions, comments, and complaints, regardless of the source.

i. I have an attitude of Positive Self Expectency. I expect, with hard, smart work, that good things will happen to me.

j. I place a high value on what I do, and that will be reflected in every aspect of my school, from my logo to my business systems.

C. Strategic Planning

a. I plan my day and execute my plan each day.

b. I understand that the hardest tasks are usually those with the highest return, and I attack them daily.

c. I have an annual goal-setting program which I break down to quarterly, monthly, weekly, and daily tasks.

d. I have created a start-up expense projection and will be able to survive if expenses are twice as high as I've projected.

e. My marketing plan is weighted towards low-risk/low-cost marketing.

f. I know exactly when I will begin promoting the Black Belt Club.

g. I know exactly when I will begin promoting my Leadership Team.

h. I have a CPA and a business attorney.

i. My sales projections are conservative, and my expense projections are high.

j. I have created an extensive business plan from scratch.

D. Sales Strategies

a. I know that I will have to become an excellent sales person.

b. I know that I will not be able to delegate selling until I am so skilled at selling I can teach the skills to my staff.

c. I can articulate the benefits of martial arts for adults and children in a manner that connects emotionally with my audience.

d. I have my scripts memorized cold for:

*   Answering the question, "What do you do for a living?"
*   Answering the phone.
*   Taking a visitor on a tour of the school.
*   Performing solo demos.
*   Community presentations and speeches.
*   Introductory classes.
*   Enrollment conferences.
*   Black Belt Club upgrades.
*   Belt exam motivational speeches (more than 30 motivational speeches for martial arts are on the www.martialartsteachers.com website).

e. I understand the key statistics to track and have a system for analyzing them daily.

f. My marketing materials and logo are professionally designed.

g. I am comfortable asking people for money (Value What You Do).

h. I use a third-party billing company for tuition processing.

i. I have a gift certificate program in place to generate referrals.

j. I understand that I don't get paid until a student enrolls, and I will use a proven system for moving strangers to students and students to black belt.

E. Student Service

a. I understand that the student and parent are the most important people in the school. My school is student-centric.

b. I understand that a complaint is an opportunity to impress my client.

c. I understand the 24-hour response rule and live by it.

d. My staff will have authority to make students and parents happy without consulting me.

e. I post event and exam dates for the coming year in December or January.

f. I have a convenient method for making up missed exams.

g. I have quantifiable standards for exams, so everyone is clear on the standards of performance at each belt.

h. My school is a safe haven of positive encouragement. I do not discuss politics, religion, or negative community events in the school.

i. My school will be cleaned every day and then spot-checked throughout the evening.

j. My staff and I will work to help students and parents understand and appreciate the benefits of our training and methods. We will not assume they understand them.

F. Getting to Profits Fast

a. I have negotiated a free-rent period.

b. I understand that "any bloody fool can spend money" and will not be a "bloody fool."

c. I understand that every dollar saved is 100-percent profit.

d. I understand that wealthy people collect interest, while poor people pay it. I will be wealthy, so I will pay off credit cards each month and NEVER lease anything but the space.

e. I have a separate account for retail. I deposit all revenue for retail into this account. I use an American Express card to pay all retail bills, so I am forced to pay it off each month. I build reward miles, so I can take my vacations for free.

f. I am the most expensive school in the area and worth it.

g. I will use Market Eyes in designing my system instead of Black Belt Eyes.

h. I have no debt other than my home, and I am paying that off in advance with advance principle payments each month with a separate check.

i. I understand Cash Out and Agreement Short strategies.

j. I have a goal of enrolling one person per working day, and a system for doing it.

G. How Will My School Look When It's Successful?

a. I will be personally debt free and saving over 20 percent of my income in conservative growth investment accounts.

b. My school will have a thriving Black Belt Club and Leadership Team.

c. My retail account will be in five figures within 12 months.

d. My school's billing check will pay 75 percent of my school's expenses.

e. I have a plan for purchasing this or another building.

f. I have a generous plan for helping my staff open their own schools.

g. My profit margin, not counting my salary, is 30 percent or higher.

h. My annual income is six figures and growing 20 percent per year.

i. My net worth is increasing 10 percent or more annually.

j. I will have at least two days per week off

H. What are the Key Numbers and Stats?

a. I have a bookkeeping and stat tracking system in place.

b. I know my cost per call and keep it under $20.

c. I calculate my retention every month, quarter and year.

d. I understand the future value in my school is in my receivables.

e. I understand that cash out revenue must be saved.

f. I fight to keep my profit margin over 30 percent.

g. I move at least 50 percent of my inquiries into students.

h. I use at least a half-dozen revenue streams each month.

i. I track my stats daily and have strategies to improve weak areas quickly.

j. I know what it costs me to get a new student.

I. The Core Dynamics and You

a. I can step outside my Black Belt Eyes and see my school, procedures, curriculum, and teaching methods through Market Eyes.

b. I am not dependent on my students' personal happiness for me to succeed.

c. I understand that what is important to my students may not be important to me.

d. I am not afraid to try new ideas in order to improve my school.

e. I respect my teachers but am finding my own voice. I am not trying to mimic anyone. I like my authentic self and am not afraid to respectfully express myself, even it flies in the face of tradition.

f. The reason that I am risking my time, money, and opportunities in opening this school is to build wealth for my family. I will not sacrifice my family for my students.

g. I have high esteem for the martial arts. I have worked hard to become the best teacher in this area, and my school will reflect that high value in every way.

h. I embrace short-term pain for long-term gain and will not let conflicting goals stop me.

i. I recognize that my patterns of thought and patterns of behavior define who I am and what I do, not what I say.

j. I am comfortable delegating tasks that are not what I do best so I may focus on my unique abilities and talents.

J. Are You the Right Person for This?

a. I love the martial arts. I think about them throughout the day and enjoy training and teaching a great deal.

b. If I won the lottery tomorrow, I would still teach and train.

c. I have no negative addictions or unhealthy patterns of behavior.

d. I have clear job descriptions and standards of performance for my staff so they can always answer the question, "Why are you on the payroll?"

e. My family supports me in this endeavor in every way but financially.

f. I love to learn and expand my skills in all areas of personal and professional life.

g. I know the success of this school is up to me, not the students, the location, the economy, or any other factor. If it's to be, it's up to me.

h. I am not afraid to sacrifice in the short term in order to succeed in the long term.

i. I do not absorb my friends and relationships into my world. I have healthy, respectful relationships with my friends and loved ones.

j. I know money is just a tool. I do not resent wealthy people, nor do I feel it is wrong to charge for my services.

Scoring Table

75 - 100	You are in the right business and positioned for success.
60 - 74	You still have some work to do. You may want to continue your training, save more money, and get more experience teaching.
Under 60	Odds are you are setting yourself up for failure. You may want to regroup and hone your skills for a while before making the leap into opening your own school.

John Graden At A Glance

1960 – Born December 2nd in Fort Hood, Texas Army Base

1974 – February 12, attends first white belt class with Hank Farrah and Walt Bone

1978 – June 24, earns first degree black belt. Hired as instructor for $5 a class

1982 – After Bone dies in place crash, begins teaching accredited college class

1983 – Wins first place in Korean forms, U.S. Open Karate Championships

1984 – Begins weekly workouts with Joe Lewis

1984 – Named co-captain with Ray McCallum of the USA Team on 10-day tour of Italy

1984 – *American Karate* heralds Graden as "an acknowledged karate master" at age 23

1985 – Wins silver medal at the WAKO World Championships in London

1986 – Opens USA Karate. Enrolls 125 students in first six weeks

1986 – Begins ten-year run as host of *USA Karate* television show

1987 – Serves as center judge for the 1st WAKO World Kata Championship in Munich, Germany.

1991 – Coaches U.S. Team at the World Open Tae Kwon Do Championships in England. Graden's student, Kathy Marlor, wins world title

1993 – Authors *Black Belt Management*

1994 – Creates and launches the National Association of Professional Martial Artists (NAPMA). 135 schools join within 30 days

1995 – Sells schools to focus on NAPMA

1996 – Launches *Martial Arts Professional* magazine

1996 – Hosts first NAPMA World Conference

1997 – Creates the American Council on Martial Arts (ACMA). Gives 6,000 ACMA manuals away for a $20 donation to Project Action

1998 – Authors *How to Open and Operate a Successful Martial Arts School* which, along with the *ACMA Manual* and *Black Belt Management*, is adapted as a college textbook

2002 – Profiled by *Wall Street Journal*

2003 – Inducted into the Joe Lewis Honor Roll, the highest honor in the Joe Lewis Fighting Systems. Graden is the youngest member ever inducted

2004 – Publishes first book by Joe Lewis, *How to Master Bruce Lee's Fighting System*

2004 – Launches the Martial Arts Teachers' Association (MATA)

2004 – Inducted into the Self-Publishers Hall of Fame

2005 – Inducted into the World Black Belt Living Legends Hall of Fame

2005 – Shot first set of sparring DVDs, *How to Teach Sparring* and *Counter Fighting*

2006 – Wrote and designed new book, *The Truth About the Martial Arts Business*

About John Graden

Rank: 7th Dan

Instructor: Joe Lewis

Founder – Martial Arts Teachers' Association (2004)

Founder – National Association of Professional Martial Artists (1994)

Founder – *Martial Arts Professional* Magazine (1995)

Founder – American Council on Martial Arts (1997)

Author –

The Truth About the Martial Arts Business

Black Belt Management

How to Open and Operate a Successful Martial Arts School

American Council on Martial Arts Instructor Certification Manual (co-author)

The Martial Arts Q & A Book (co-author)

Author, athlete, publisher, and pioneering martial arts visionary, John Graden, is widely recognized as the most important martial arts leader to emerge in the 1990s.

His efforts as a "teacher of teachers" have had a profound impact on the manner in which thousands of martial arts schools are operated worldwide. A former member of many world champion U.S. kickboxing teams, Graden's two top-selling books, *Black Belt Management* and *How To Open and Operate A Successful Martial Arts School*, are considered the quintessential references for martial arts school owners. His new book, *The Truth About the Martial Arts Business* is hailed as an instant classic.

In late 1994, Graden founded the National Association of Professional Martial Artists (NAPMA). Dedicated specifically to strengthening the professional skills of martial arts school owners, NAPMA mushroomed to more than 2,000 members worldwide making it the largest martial arts professional association in the world.

In 1995, he strengthened his position as a martial arts teacher of teachers by launching *Martial Arts Professional* magazine, the martial arts trade journal.

In an effort to present universal instructor education to the martial arts industry, Graden created the American Council on Martial Arts (ACMA) in 1997. The ACMA was the first widely supported instructor certification program and was administered by the world renowned Cooper Institute in Dallas, Texas. The manual for the ACMA has been adapted as a textbook in colleges and universities. The ACMA is now the Martial Arts Teachers' Association Instructor Certification Program at MartialArtsTeachers.com.

Graden is a seventh degree black belt under Lewis and is the youngest man ever named to the Joe Lewis Honor Roll, the highest honor in the Joe Lewis Fighting System.

Graden now serves as the Executive Director of the Martial Arts Teachers' Association. Due to its global reach, Graden considers MATA to be his most important work.

The worldwide headquarters of MATA is at www.MartialArtsTeachers.com and offers a massive library of articles, information, reports, videos, audios, ads, newsletters, forms, letters and networking to martial arts instructors worldwide.

Graden is married with two children and lives in Palm Harbor, Florida. Mr. Graden can be reached at johngraden@martialartsteachers.com.

Retail Sales Breakthrough

New online proshop allows martial arts schools to double and even triple their current retail sales.

Retail sales are a pain. Stocking inventory, asking for orders, giving out catalogs and order forms, spending class time collecting money, placing the orders with the supply company, waiting for the UPS guy, unpacking and sorting, and finally handing out the equipment to students. It just doesn't seem worth the effort beyond uniforms and gear. Until now.

PERFECT RETAIL SOLUTION

You are now able to earn more revenue and save thousands of dollars with a new online proshop designed by Webmation. Take orders 24 hours a day, offer thousands of martial arts related products, run holiday specials and promotions, give discounts to black belt club members and the demo team, and even accept online payments for testing fees, school events, seminars, summer camp and more.

QUICK AND EASY

You choose which products you want to include, set the price and still only pay your regular wholesale rates. Setting up the proshop is easy with an online control panel that lets you make changes to your proshop instantaneously.

When a student orders from your proshop, the money goes straight into your bank account, you are billed wholesale and the order is shipped directly to your student.

WIDE PRODUCT SELECTION

Offer any of Tiger Claw's thousands of products including uniforms, apparel, sparring equipment, training tools and weapons in your propshop. Even items such as keychains, patches, belt displays, rebreakable bricks and real wood boards are available for your students to buy from your proshop.

ON-DEMAND LOGO CUSTOMIZATION

Not only can you include your logo on sparring gear, uniforms, training equipment and a full apparel line - you can do so without buying in bulk, order minimums or stocking inventory! That means if a student wants to go to your online proshop and order one school sweatshirt, they can!

Boost your proshop sales by offering over 387 school branded fitness apparel items in your proshop. A create your own clothing line feature also allows students to design their own items. No order minimums, stocking inventory or ordering in bulk needed.

PROSHOP FEATURES

In addition to being able to offer over 20 different kind of promotions and discounts, you can create bundle packs and send email coupons through the Webmation E-mailer system that include Tiger Claw's professional product shots.

MANY MORE WAYS TO MAKE MONEY

You will also save on inventory taxes, sales tax (except TN and CA), shipping costs and have more time to focus on more important areas of your school.

The online proshop is just one revenue generating component of the Ultimate Martial Arts Internet System. To request a free information kit, visit www.webmation.com or call our 24 hour toll free request line at 1-866-521-7177.

WEBMATION®

The Truth About the
Martial Arts Business